His classic first law—"Work expands so as to fill the time available"—is generally acknowledged to be as true as the Law of Gravity.

His latest law, the Law of the Vacuum—"Action expands to fill the void created by human failure"—is probably the most comprehensive explanation of human behavior to date.

Here is *all* of Parkinson, supreme sage for a world helplessly ensnared in corporate and government red tape. It is the very best of Parkinson and Parkinson at his best.

"PARKINSON WILL TELL TRUTH . . . CLEAR AND FUNNY."
The New York Times
Book Review

PARKINSON: THE LAW,
COMPLETE

C. Northcote Parkinson

Illustrated by Osbert Lancaster

BALLANTINE BOOKS • NEW YORK

FOR ANN

Contents

SOURCES
Chapters 1, 4, 7, 9, 12, 13, 14 and 15 are from *Parkinson's Law* (1958); 2, 10 and 11 are from *The Law of Delay* (1970); 3, 5 and 6 are from *The Law and the Profits* (1960); and 8 is from *In-Laws and Outlaws* (1962).

Foreword

Parkinson's Law had a considerable impact at the time it was first published and was widely discussed. Its readers were made aware of some human characteristics which had never before been precisely described. Previously known facts were fitted into a new pattern and many people had a sense of relief in finding that ideas, long vaguely present in the mind, had at last been put into words. Parkinson's Law had been discovered, remember, not invented, and the author could place himself (modestly, of course) on a level with Archimedes, Pythagoras and Newton. The purpose of that book was almost purely satirical and it is the nature of satire to reveal sad truth without suggesting a remedy. The validity of Parkinson's Law has been proved again and again. For that reason the original chapter is here reprinted without amendment.

I followed *Parkinson's Law* with a number of other studies seeking to establish similar principles in related fields of administration. Over the years a new generation has grown up for whom my Laws are known by name and perhaps, at least vaguely, as ideas, but of those who quote or misquote them only a few have read them. I suggest that after twenty-one years, while the message is the same, the predictions have been verified. Some businessmen and some shareholders have made a profit from this discovery and others will do so again. But such gains are as nothing compared with the savings which might still be made in the public sector. If countries were lightened of their tax burdens, relieved of excessive bureaucracy, and cured of administrative constipation, we should see a sudden outburst of real activity and enterprise. In hopes of this I have gathered my Laws together in one volume for the first time and laid them once more before the public, amplified wherever possible by more recent findings.

During the years I have been writing it has been borne in upon me that underlying my Laws in various fields there is a more fundamental and larger Law that unites them, a Law that goes far to explain the situation of the present world both in commerce and in politics. For those who already know my writings it may be instructive to read them again in a new and broader light. There is a widely accepted scientific principle that nature abhors a vacuum; it manifests itself in many ways, some of which have proved of great benefit to man. I now offer it for consideration that the field of human affairs provides some of the richest examples of this principle in action, and in my concluding chapter I have attempted to formulate once again a Law for our times—one which may appear obvious but which, as far as I know, has never hitherto been recognised.

C. Northcote Parkinson
1979

GOVERNMENT

I

Parkinson's Law
or The Rising Pyramid

WORK EXPANDS SO AS TO FILL THE TIME AVAILABLE FOR
its completion. General recognition of this fact is shown in
the proverbial phrase 'It is the busiest man who has time to
spare.' Thus, an elderly lady of leisure can spend the entire
day in writing and dispatching a postcard to her niece at
Bognor Regis. An hour will be spent in finding the postcard, another in hunting for spectacles, half an hour in a
search for the address, an hour and a quarter in composition, and twenty minutes in deciding whether or not to take
an umbrella when going to the pillar box in the next street.
The total effort that would occupy a busy man for three
minutes all told may in this fashion leave another person
prostrate after a day of doubt, anxiety, and toil.

Granted that work (and especially paperwork) is thus
elastic in its demands on time, it is manifest that there
need be little or no relationship between the work to be
done and the size of the staff to which it may be assigned.

A lack of real activity does not, of necessity, result in leisure. A lack of occupation is not necessarily revealed by a manifest idleness. The thing to be done swells in importance and complexity in a direct ratio with the time to be spent. This fact is widely recognised, but less attention has been paid to its wider implications, more especially in the field of public administration. Politicians and taxpayers have assumed (with occasional phases of doubt) that a rising total in the number of civil servants must reflect a growing volume of work to be done. Cynics, in questioning this belief, have imagined that the multiplication of officials must have left some of them idle or all of them able to work for shorter hours. But this is a matter in which faith and doubt seem equally misplaced. The fact is that the number of the officials and the quantity of the work are not related to each other at all. The rise in the total of those employed is governed by Parkinson's Law and would be much the same whether the volume of the work were to increase, diminish, or even disappear. The importance of Parkinson's Law lies in the fact that it is a law of growth based upon an analysis of the factors by which that growth is controlled.

The validity of this recently discovered law must rest mainly on statistical proofs, which will follow. Of more interest to the general reader is the explanation of the factors underlying the general tendency to which this law gives definition. Omitting technicalities (which are numerous) we may distinguish at the outset two motive forces. They can be represented for the present purpose by two almost axiomatic statements, thus: (1) 'An official wants to multiply subordinates, not rivals' and (2) 'Officials make work for each other.'

To comprehend Factor 1, we must picture a civil servant, called A, who finds himself overworked. Whether this overwork is real or imaginary is immaterial, but we should observe, in passing, that A's sensation (or illusion) might easily result from his own decreasing energy: a normal symptom of middle age. For this real or imagined overwork there are, broadly speaking, three possible remedies. He may resign; he may ask to halve the work with a colleague called B; he may demand the assistance of two subordinates, to be called C and D. There is probably no instance, however, in history of A choosing any but the third alternative. By resignation he would lose his pension rights. By having B appointed, on his own level in the hierarchy, he would merely bring in a rival for promotion to W's vacancy when W (at long last) retires. So A would rather have C and D, junior men, below him. They will add to his consequence and, by dividing the work into two categories, as between C and D, he will have the merit of being the only man who comprehends them both. It is essential to realise at this point that C and D are, as it were, inseparable. To appoint C alone would have been impossible. Why? Because C, if by himself, would divide the work with A and so assume almost the equal status that has been refused in the first instance to B; a status the more emphasised if C is A's only possible successor. Subordinates must thus number two or more, each being thus kept in order by fear of the other's promotion. When C complains in turn of being overworked (as he certainly will) A will, with the concurrence of C, advise the appointment of two assistants to help C. But he can then avert internal friction only by advising the appointment of two more assistants to help D, whose position is much the same. With this recruitment of E, F, G, and H the promotion of A is now practically certain.

Seven officials are now doing what one did before. This is where Factor 2 comes into operation. For these seven make so much work for each other that all are fully occupied and A is actually working harder than ever. An incoming document may well come before each of them in turn. Official E decides that it falls within the province of F, who places a draft reply before C, who amends it drastically before consulting D, who asks G to deal with it. But G goes on leave at this point, handing the file over to H, who drafts a minute that is signed by D and returned to C, who revises his draft accordingly and lays the new version before A.

What does A do? He would have every excuse for signing the thing unread, for he has many other matters on his mind. Knowing now that he is to succeed W next year, he has to decide whether C or D should succeed to his own office. He had to agree to G's going on leave even if not yet strictly entitled to it. He is worried whether H should not have gone instead, for reasons of health. He has looked pale recently—partly but not solely because of his domestic troubles. Then there is the business of F's special increment of salary for the period of the conference and E's application for transfer to the Ministry of Pensions. A has heard that D is in love with a married typist and that G and F are no longer on speaking terms—no one seems to know why. So A might be tempted to sign C's draft and have done with it. But A is a conscientious man. Beset as he is with problems created by his colleagues for them- selves and for him—created by the mere fact of these officials' existence—he is not the man to shirk his duty. He reads through the draft with care, deletes the fussy paragraphs added by C and H, and restores the thing to the form preferred in the first instance by the able (if quarrel- some) F. He corrects the English—none of these young men can write grammatically—and finally produces the same reply he would have written if officials C to H had never been born. Far more people have taken far longer to produce the same result. No one has been idle. All have done their best. And it is late in the evening before A finally quits his office and begins the return journey to Ealing. The last of the office lights are being turned off in the gathering dusk that marks the end of another day's administrative toil. Among the last to leave, A reflects with bowed shoulders and a wry smile that late hours, like grey hairs, are among the penalties of success.

From this description of the factors at work the student of political science will recognise that administrators are more or less bound to multiply. Nothing has yet been said, however, about the period of time likely to elapse between the date of A's appointment and the date from which we can calculate the pensionable service of H. Vast masses of statistical evidence have been collected and it is from a

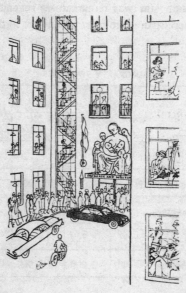

study of this data that Parkinson's Law has been deduced. Space will not allow of detailed analysis but the reader will be interested to know that research began in the Navy Estimates. These were chosen because the Admiralty's responsibilities are more easily measurable than those of, say, the Board of Trade. The question is merely one of numbers and tonnage. Here are some typical figures. The strength of the Navy in 1914 could be shown as 146,000 officers and men, 3,249 dockyard officials and clerks, and 57,000 dockyard workmen. By 1928 there were only 100,000 officers and men and only 62,439 workmen, but the dockyard officials and clerks by then numbered 4,558. As for warships, the strength in 1928 was a mere fraction of what it had been in 1914—fewer than 20 capital ships in commission as compared with 62. Over the same period the Admiralty officials had increased in number from 2,000 to 3,569, providing (as was remarked) 'a magnificent navy on land.' These figures are more clearly set forth in tabular form:

ADMIRALTY STATISTICS

Classification	Year		Increase or Decrease %
	1914	1928	
Capital ships in commission	62	20	−67.74
Officers and men in RN	146,000	100,000	−31.5
Dockyard workers	57,000	62,439	+9.54
Dockyard officials and clerks	3,249	4,558	+40.28
Admiralty officials	2,000	3,569	+78.45

The criticism voiced at the time centred on the ratio between the number of those available for fighting and those available only for administration. But that comparison is not to the present purpose. What we have to note is that the 2,000 officials of 1914 had become the 3,569 of 1928; and that this growth was unrelated to any possible increase in their work. The Navy during that period had diminished, in point of fact, by a third in men and two-thirds in ships. Nor, from 1922 onward, was its strength even expected to increase; for its total of ships (unlike its total of officials) was limited by the Washington Naval Agreement of that year. Here we have then a 78 per cent increase over a period of fourteen years; an average of 5.6 per cent increase a year on the earlier total. In fact, as we shall see, the rate of increase was not as regular as that. All we have to consider, at this stage, is the percentage rise over a given period.

Can this rise in the total number of civil servants be accounted for except on the assumption that such a total must always rise by a law governing its growth? It might be urged at this point that the period under discussion was one of rapid development in naval technique. The use of the flying machine was no longer confined to the eccentric. Electrical devices were being multiplied and elaborated. Submarines were tolerated if not approved. Engineer officers were beginning to be regarded as almost human. In so revolutionary an age we might expect that storekeepers would have more elaborate inventories to compile. We might not wonder to see more draughtsmen on the payroll, more designers, more technicians and scientists. But these, the dockyard officials, increased only by 40 per cent in number when the men of Whitehall increased their total by nearly 80 per cent. For every new foreman or electrical engineer at Portsmouth there had to be two more clerks at

Charing Cross. From this we might be tempted to conclude, provisionally, that the rate of increase in administrative staff is likely to be double that of the technical staff at a time when the actually useful strength (in this case, of seamen) is being reduced by 31.5 per cent. It has been proved statistically, however, that this last percentage is irrelevant. The officials would have multiplied at the same rate had there been no actual seamen at all.

It would be interesting to follow the further progress by which the 8,118 Admiralty staff of 1935 came to number 33,788 by 1954. But the staff of the Colonial Office affords a better field of study during a period of imperial decline. Admiralty statistics are complicated by factors (like the Fleet Air Arm) that make comparison difficult as between one year and the next. The Colonial Office growth is more significant in that it is more purely administrative. Here the relevant statistics are as follows:

COLONIAL OFFICE STATISTICS

Year	1935	1939	1943	1947	1954
Staff	372	450	817	1,139	1,661

Before showing what the rate of increase is, we must observe that the extent of this department's responsibilities was far from constant during these twenty years. The colonial territories were not much altered in area or population between 1935 and 1939. They were considerably diminished by 1943, certain areas being in enemy hands. They were increased again in 1947, but have since then shrunk steadily from year to year as successive colonies achieve self-government. It would be rational to suppose that these changes in the scope of Empire would be reflected in the size of its central administration. But a glance at the figures is enough to convince us that the staff totals represent nothing but so many stages in an inevitable increase. And this increase, although related to that observed in other departments, has nothing to do with the size—or even the existence—of the Empire. What are the percentages of increase? We must ignore, for this purpose, the rapid increase in staff which accompanied the diminution of responsibility during World War II. We should note rather, the peacetime rates of increase: over 5.24 per cent between 1935 and 1939, and 6.55 per cent between 1947 and 1954. This gives an average increase of 5.89 per cent each year, a percentage markedly similar to that already found in the Admiralty staff increase between 1914 and 1928.

Further and detailed statistical analysis of departmental staffs would be inappropriate in such a work as this. It is hoped, however, to reach a tentative conclusion regarding the time likely to elapse between a given official's first appointment and the later appointment of his two or more assistants.

Dealing with the problem of pure staff accumulation, all our researches so far completed point to an average increase of 5.75 per cent per year. This fact established, it now becomes possible to state Parkinson's Law in mathematical form: In any public administrative department not actually at war, the staff increase may be expected to follow this formula:

$$x = \frac{2k^m + l}{n}$$

where k is the number of staff seeking promotion through the appointment of subordinates; l represents the difference between the ages of appointment and retirement; m is the number of man-hours devoted to answering minutes within the department; and n is the number of effective units being administered, x will be the number of new staff required each year. Mathematicians will, of course, realise that to find the percentage increase they must multiply x by 100 and divide the total of the previous year (y), thus:

$$\frac{100\,(2k^m + l)}{yn}\%$$

And this figure will invariably prove to be between 5.17 per cent and 6.56 per cent, irrespective of any variation in the amount of work (if any) to be done.

The discovery of this formula and of the general principles upon which it is based has, of course, no political value. No attempt has been made to inquire whether departments *ought* to grow in size. Those who hold that this growth is essential to gain full employment are fully entitled to their opinion. Those who doubt the stability of an economy based upon reading each other's minutes are equally entitled to theirs. It would probably be premature to attempt at this stage any inquiry into the quantitative ratio that should exist between the administrators and the administered. Granted, however, that a maximum ratio exists, it should soon be possible to ascertain by formula how many years will elapse before that ratio, in any given community, will be reached. The forecasting of such a result will again have no political value. Nor can it be sufficiently emphasised that Parkinson's Law is a purely scientific discovery, inapplicable except in theory to the politics of the day. It is not the business of the botanist to eradicate the weeds. Enough for him if he can tell us just how fast they grow.

2

Twenty-One Years After or Higher and Wider

TWENTY-ONE YEARS HAVE PASSED AND IT IS FAIR TO ASK what the position is now? Do the statistics of the past decade go to substantiate or undermine the theory first propounded? This question is not easy to answer for official statistics are inconsistent, complex, and obscure. There have been frequent reorganisations in which responsibilities and manpower have been shuffled around the Foreign and Commonwealth Office. There has been the merger of the Armed Forces and of the Consular with the Diplomatic Corps. To discover what has happened is no easy task. Nor has the situation been unaffected by the author himself. If Karl Marx's predictions were falsified, in part, because his opponents had read his book, it may be true that *Parkinson's Law* has influenced the Select Committee on Estimates. Despite all confusion, however, and despite the impact of the book (as contrasted with the Law) there are grounds for regarding the author as a true prophet.

Take the Admiralty, to begin with, as our first and classic example of administrative proliferation (*see below*). The conclusion from this research would be that the 5.5 per cent growth of the Admiralty staff (calculated arithmetically on the base year) between 1914 and 1928 was replaced by a 9.3 per cent growth between 1938 and 1958, and whereas 1914 represented the culmination of an arms race, when 4,366 officials could administer what was then the largest navy in the world, 1967 represented the point at which we became practically powerless, by which period over 33,000 civil servants are barely sufficient to administer the navy we no longer possess. Negligible as we may be in world politics, we can still deploy administrative forces in Bath, Whitehall, Queen Anne's Mansions, Rex House, Kidbrooke, Cricklewood, Harrow, and the Charing Cross Road. For any weakness observable at Singapore or Malta we may console ourselves with the thought that our base at Northwood Hills (Pinner) is virtually impregnable.

The Law

	1914	1928	Increase or Decrease
Total number of vessels in commission	542	317	−41.51%
Officers and men in RN	125,000	90,700	−27.44%
Dockyard workers	57,000	62,439	+9.54%
Dockyard officials and clerical staff	3,249	4,558	+40.28%
Admiralty officials and clerical staff	4,366	7,729	+77.03%

[The subsequent story, up to the merger and for a later year (1967), *would read as follows]*

	1938	1948	1958	1964	1967
Total number of vessels	308	413	238	182	114
Officers and men	89,500	134,400	94,900	84,900	83,900
Dockyard workers	39,022	48,252	40,164	41,563	37,798
Dockyard officials and clerical staff	4,423	6,120	6,219	7,395	8,013
Admiralty officials and clerical staff	11,270	31,636	32,237	32,035	33,574

It would be interesting to follow the further progress by which the 8,118 Admiralty staff of 1935 came to number 33,788 by 1954. But, remote as the administrators may be from the sea, they would seem to have studied the habits of the cuttle fish, which confuses its pursuers by the ejection of ink. Many of the clerical staff may actually have met a seaman moreover in the course of their career and heard him say, 'When in trouble, make smoke.' The result is that shiftings of responsibility and changes of title have made all further comparisons difficult or impossible. We know, for example, that the ships in commission (most of them quite small and hardly any to be classed as capital) numbered 166 by 1968, manned by 85,940 officers and men, and assisted by 5,938 dockyard officials and 52,109 dockyard workers. The number of greatest interest here is that of the dockyard officials, multiplying inexorably against a background of dwindling strength. As from about then the scene is obscured by clouds of ink with new distinctions drawn between industrial and non-industrial workers, between both and such other men as are employed on repair and maintenance. As for the Admiralty staff it has vanished within the tangled thickets of the Ministry of Defence.

It would be wrong, incidentally, to suppose that the Naval Division of the Ministry of Defence brought to that headquarters a habit of administrative expansion which was alien to the other Services. The War Office, for one, need never shirk comparison with the Admiralty. In 1935 a civilian staff of 9,442 sufficed to administer an Army reduced to 203,361 officers and men; the low-water mark of unpreparedness for a conflict which was by then obviously inevitable. By 1966 a civilian staff of 48,032 was giving encouragement to some 187,100 men in uniform, a 7.9 per cent reduction in fighting strength being accompanied by a 408 per cent increase in paperwork. It might be rash, however, to surmise that an annual 13.16 per cent increase in civilian staff is normal to the War Office. We have rather to realise that merger with Navy and Air Force tripled the volume of correspondence as from the first day and that further progression is more likely to be on a geometric than on a merely arithmetic scale. If we thus plot on a graph the curve of expansion for the Admiralty Division of the Ministry of Defence we find that its civilian staff should number about 72,000 by 1984,* in which year there should of course be no Navy of any kind. By the same year the military division of the same Ministry should number about 124,000.

Our second example of administrative growth was taken

* Why 1984? Why not?

16

from the Colonial Office, the figures quoted being as follows:

1935	1939	1943	1947	1954
173	450	817	1,139	1,661

For the same years the combined total of the Colonial, Dominion, India, and Burma Offices was as follows:

1,023	1,075	1,709	2,362	2,650

Various reorganisations prevent us giving any more recent totals than for 1957 (2,743) and for 1960 (2,827). We need to remember, however, that the period covered by these statistics, from 1935 to the present day, is notable for the collapse of our empire; a collapse for which there is hardly a parallel in history. From 1947, more especially, we can list as follows the territories which gained their independence: India, Pakistan, Ceylon, Ghana, Malaysia, Cyprus, Nigeria, Sierra Leone, Tanzania, Jamaica, Trinidad and Tobago, Uganda, Kenya, Malawi, Malta, Zambia, Gambia, Singapore, Guyana, Botswana, Lesotho, and Barbados. Confusion surrounds the totals employed in the Colonial, Dominion, India, and Burma Offices and while we must wonder a little at the 10,615 people employed by the Foreign and Commonwealth Office by 1970, we find that our more detailed analysis is lost in a misty borderland of shifting definitions and varying totals.

Each newly independent territory has meant the loss of a governorship and the gain of an embassy. Whereas our ambassadors numbered only 16 in 1940 they now number over 80 with High Commissioners as well and representatives accredited to NATO, SEATO, and UNO. A 412.5 per cent increase in the number of embassies might seem to justify a 378.23 per cent increase in the staff of the Foreign Service. Whether that was the actual increase must remain doubtful however, because there are, in this instance, four different sets of figures to choose from; one from the Treasury, one from the Foreign Office News Department, another from Civil Estimates, and the last from the Diplomatic Service Administration Office. Of these guesses the first has been preferred but it differs from the last by about 7,000. Whether those employed in Whitehall have ever been actually counted must remain a question and it is just as difficult to obtain a precise estimate of those recruited locally overseas. In so far, however, as the figures can be trusted at all, the Foreign Office/Diplomatic Service would seem to have been heavily reinforced since 1940, the following figures giving at least a vague indication of the recent trend:

1935	1940	1945	1950	1955	1960	1965	1967
1,412	2,270	6,806	6,195	5,670	5,992	10,211	10,856

The sudden increase recorded for 1965 was not due to a diplomatic crisis but to an amalgamation with the Commonwealth Relations Office, which had itself risen in strength from 651 (in 1935) to 1,729 (in 1964). Such reorganisations apart, the tale of expansion is highly impressive. If mere numbers could achieve anything, our current representation overseas should signify an almost overwhelming influence on world affairs.

From the varying and dubious figures we have quoted it

will appear that Parkinson's Law has not been disproved over the past decade; least of all, perhaps, in the Ministries to which the author first drew attention. The trend of inevitable increase is certainly proved from British experience. What is more doubtful is the preliminary guess that annual peacetime staff accumulation may average 5.75 per cent. This prediction was qualified, remember, by the reminder that 'new developments occur almost daily' and that all estimates be regarded as tentative. Granted that this is so, and that further research remains to be done, the fact remains that the author's first guess was not too wide of the mark. Whereas the Ministries vary in their rate of staff accumulation, the average annual increase in five of them would work out as shown in the table opposite for the period 1935–66.

Of this increase, however, a part is attributable to an actual increase of work. The population of Britain rose from 45,598,000 in 1935 to 53,266,000 in 1966, justifying a 16.8 per cent increase in the cost of administration, an annual increase of 0.5 per cent per year. Taxation was made steadily more onerous and complex and bureaucratic interference with trade became habitual. We are frequently at war on a minor scale and the financial problem of reconciling this with vote-catching welfare measures made perpetual difficulties for the Civil Service. With more people in prison for contravening more obscure laws and regulations there was bound to be more work for the Home Office. In this way perhaps half of the annual increase might be explained, leaving 4.34 per cent to be accounted for by the operation of Parkinson's Law. This falls short of the original estimate but we have to remember that Ministries have not merely grown but multiplied. The modest growth of the Board of Trade is thus due to the establishment of the parallel Ministries of Transport and Technology. If allowance is made for these developments, the inevitable growth—apart from any increases in work-load—may turn out to be very near the 5.75 per cent of the original estimate. It will be manifest, however, that exact figures and percentages are almost unattainable.

Ministry	1935	1966	% annual increase
Home Office and Prison Commission	4,350	16,066	8.68
Inland Revenue	22,851	59,502	5.17
War Office	9,442	48,032	13.18
Board of Trade	4,328	9,598	3.92
Air Ministry	5,481	24,848	11.39
Average annual increase			8.49

What, however, of the Civil Service as a whole? Here again there are statistical difficulties due to reorganisation and shifting areas of responsibility. There is a confused boundary between central and local government and a misty borderland between public service and nationalised industry. To make matters even more obscure there is no immutable distinction between industrial and nonindustrial staff, a mere reclassification of grades in the Post Office being enough to alter the total by thousands. Within these shifting frontiers, however, the statistics—for what they are worth—read somewhat as follows:

1935	1940	1945	1950	1955	1960	1965
303,610	454,745	704,646	684,799	635,663	637,374	803,327

GOVERNMENT

As on 1 January 1967 the total was 845,900, a not unimpressive share of the working population. This represents a 179 per cent increase over the 32-year period or an annual average increase of 5.6 per cent. That the percentage is not higher than that is due, in the first place, to the more modest demands of certain Ministries. That of Labour and National Service, for example, has actually declined since 1935 and nearly halved since 1943, much of its work being taken over by the Ministry of National Insurance. The Ministry of Transport has also halved since 1959. Such restraint, however, as there has been in other directions has been the result, clearly, of Parkinson's Law becoming known. The total of civil servants was actually reduced in 1955—the year in which the essay first appeared—and was reduced again after the discovery was published in book form. Expansion began once more in 1960–5, after the initial impact of the book had been spent, and has continued ever since.

In the original essay (which first appeared in *The Economist* in 1955) much emphasis was placed on the purely scientific nature of the discovery there revealed, the author going so far as to observe that, 'It is not the business of the botanist to eradicate the weeds. Enough for him if he can tell us just how fast they grow.' It is surely appropriate that the present inquiry should be pursued in the same objective spirit. No attempt will be made, therefore, to decide whether 845,900 civil servants are too many or too few. We are justified, however, in plotting a curve to show what the result of the present rate of growth might be. By what date, we can fairly ask, should half the working population be absorbed in public administration? By what date, further, should the *whole* population have been so absorbed? For this purpose we need to include those employed in local as well as national affairs; a total of 1,077,050 public servants at the present time. Estimates reveal that these two dates are 2145 and 2195 respectively. It is no part of our present object to comment upon the new type of economy which will support such a way of life. That people should live by reading each other's memoranda is regarded, in official circles, as perfectly natural and feasible. There can be no doubt that the main features of the new economy have been foreseen and that planners are already studying their manifold implications. It is not for the private citizen, however, to venture into these realms of speculation. There are large and expanding departments devoted to blue-printing the coming Utopia and the whole subject is better left, therefore, to the experts.

Central to our system of administration and foremost in the march of progress is, of course, the Treasury. It is the Treasury that watches over the whole structure, ensuring

that nothing is spent which could be saved and that nobody is employed whose services are not essential. Some comment upon the Treasury is to that extent inevitable and is the more needed in that one's mental picture of that institution is probably false. We think of the Treasury as comprising a small group of the dedicated and erudite, all from Winchester and New College and a few with some experience of the 60th Rifles. These are men, we imagine, of classical education whose subparagraphs are distinguished by letters from the Greek alphabet. They lunch at the Reform and do *The Times* crossword puzzle in a matter of seconds. They spend their evenings listening to classical music, their weekends at home in Hampstead Garden Suburb. They are, we tend to believe, at once powerful and obscure. Knowing that there are supposed to be about 200 of them, we may feel, as taxpayers, that never in the history of human extortion has so much been owed by so many to so few. Our preconceptions are largely based, however, upon errors of fact, and one such error concerns the numbers of the Treasury staff. This central Ministry may be small as compared with others but it is inferior to few in its speed of growth. The following figures may suffice to prove this point:

1940	1945	1950	1955	1960	1965
378	818	1,414	1,312	1,340	1,584

This multiplication of the available financial talent over twenty-five years is not unimpressive during a period of a country's steady decline. There were, it is true, some carping critics who asked why few if any of the officials had any qualifications in accountancy, but this question was very properly ignored. As against that, it was agreed in 1968 that the financial supervisors did themselves require supervision. The result was to establish a new Civil Service Department, a Super Supervisory hierarchy which itself multiplied from 2,103 in 1970 to 5,256 in 1975—a growth-rate which is believed to represent a world record. Adding the super-supervisors to the supervisors we had the impressive total of 6,321 by 1975, a year in which the country was practically bankrupt.

Among the old-established Ministries whose functions have not vastly altered only one, the War Office (with a 13.18 per cent increase per annum), can claim any comparable progress. If we ignore some recent developments in technological fields, we must conclude that the Treasury leads the way. When we realise moreover that there has been a parallel growth of other offices concerned with finance, from the Ministry of Economic Affairs* to the nationalised Bank of England, we might feel justified in making a total for them all. Such a calculation would place the Treasury far ahead of the field and in a class by itself.

While we find that Ministries themselves are apt to change their names and functions, making comparisons meaningless, we can still regard as significant the total of those on the public payroll, whether industrial or nonindustrial, a figure of 702,056 in 1970 becoming greater than 746,000 by 1977. To complete the picture we need to add the total of those employed by local government. Some idea is conveyed by the table which follows, covering the period from 1960 to 1977:

* Now part of the Treasury.

GOVERNMENT

1960	1,709,000	1969	2,344,000
1961	1,755,000	1970	2,386,000
1962	1,821,000	1971	2,466,000
1963	1,887,000	1972	2,584,000
1964	1,964,000	1973	2,699,000
1965	2,025,000	1974	2,697,000
1966	2,123,000	1975	2,893,000
1967	2,212,000	1976	2,939,000
1968	2,287,000	1977	2,911,000

While the Treasury has failed to hold down the numbers of the Civil Service, and has by its example encouraged proliferation, it has admittedly done something to limit the rising cost. The fact that the top civil servants have demanded, and obtained, something like the salaries paid to their industrial opposite numbers must not conceal from us the fact that their underlings are rather underpaid than otherwise. It is true that the total salary payments rose from £298 million in 1951 to £773 million in 1965. It is arguable, however, that the increase for the individual has barely kept pace with the dwindling value of the currency. Was the average pay per head in 1951 (£440) fairly represented, in purchasing power, by the average pay of 1965? This came to £1,057 and it offered, as an average, something very far short of wealth. Any industrial consultant might consider that double the salary would obtain more useful work from a quarter the number. That, however, is not to the present purpose, which is merely to record that the Treasury, failing dismally to restrain the rise in numbers, *can* claim a modest success in limiting the expense.

What, then, are we to think of the original prophecy? Civil servants *do* multiply by a law which governs their department's expansion. Work *does* expand so as to fill the time available. Nor does the fact that people are busy prove that there is anything useful for them to do. We have no statistical proof, however, for the theory that 5–6 per cent per annum is the normal rate of staff-accumulation. It is not wildly off the mark but the variations from this norm are at once frequent and unpredictable. It was the fashion among the early economists to explain what would happen in certain circumstances, a shortage causing a rise in price, a slack period causing a fall in wages. All these rules applied only to a free market, unaffected by governmental action or by combinations in restraint of trade; free, moreover, from civil disturbance or war. In the 20th century the right circumstances never exist. There is a sense in which Parkinson's Law (or, to be exact, his first law) has suffered the same fate. The author postulated (very tentatively) a certain rate of administrative expansion in time of peace. He assumed the absence of any financial crisis or internal revolution. It is a question whether these conditions have prevailed over the twenty-one years we are considering or are likely to prevail over the twenty-one years ahead. This is not an age to which any very precise rules can be made to apply, least of all when the rules themselves have become generally known. His failure was in neglecting to make any allowance for the impact the theory was actually to have. Granted, however, that the Whitehall scene is confused by this factor among others, the basic fact remains that London (like Vienna) is now the disproportionately large capital of an empire that has ceased to exist. The headquarters of government was never designed as the administrative hub of the British Isles but as the centre of a spider's web which used to cover half the world. With that larger function gone, the Whitehall of today is not merely cumbersome but ludicrous. Reform may be impossible but we have still (so far) the right at least to laugh.

3

Law of Extravagance
or Expense no Object

EXPENDITURE RISES TO MEET INCOME. PARKINSON'S SEC-
ond Law, like the first, is a matter of everyday experience, manifest as soon as it is stated, as obvious as it is
simple. When the individual has a rise in salary, he and his
wife are prone to decide how the additional income is to be
spent: so much on an insurance policy, so much to the
savings bank, so much in a trust fund for the children.
They might just as well save themselves the trouble, for no
surplus ever comes into view. The extra salary is silently
absorbed, leaving the family barely in credit and often, in
fact, with a deficit which has actually increased. Individual
expenditure not only rises to meet income but tends to
surpass it, and probably always will.

It is less widely recognised that what is true of individuals is also true of governments. Whatever the revenue may
be, there will always be the pressing need to spend it. But
between governments and individuals there is this vital

difference, that the government rarely pauses even to consider what its income is. Were any of us to adopt the methods of public finance in our private affairs we should ignore the total of our income and consider only what we should like to spend. We might decide on a second car, an extension of the home, a motor launch as well as a yacht, a country place in the Cotswolds, and a long holiday in Bermuda. All these, we should tell each other, are essential. It would remain only to adjust our income to cover these bare necessities; and if we economise at all, it will be in matters of taxation. A government, by contrast, which applied the methods of individual finance to public expenditure would begin by attempting to estimate what its actual revenue should be. Given so much to spend, how much should be allocated to what? A government which decided upon this novel approach to the subject would be responsible for a revolution in public finance. It is the chief object of this chapter to suggest that such a revolution is overdue.

Governmental as opposed to individual income is historically linked with the incidence of war. In all systems of revenue there has always been provision for the temporary expenses of conflict. During a time of emergency, with our interests, our beliefs, our pride, or even our existence at stake, we agree to pay almost anything as the price of victory. The war ends and with it the temporary expenses which everyone has seen to be more or less inevitable. In theory the revenue should fall to something like its previous level. In practice it seldom does. While the governmental income remains almost at its wartime level, peacetime expenditure rises to meet it. In times past the action of this law was slightly restrained, to be sure, by two considerations which no longer apply. In the first place, it was usually felt that taxes had to be reduced somewhat in time of peace in order to allow for their being raised again in time of war. During a century, however, when each successive war is judged to be the last, this theory finds no further support. In the second place, there are types of extravagance which yield only a diminishing return. To the provision of banquets and the enjoyment of dancing girls there is (eventually) a physical limit. The same is not true, unfortunately, of departmental and technical luxuriance. Economic and cultural advisers can multiply beyond the point at which concubines might be thought a bore; beyond the point even at which they might be thought unbearable. Financially as well as aesthetically, the situation has become infinitely worse.

In countries like Britain and the United States the initiative in public finance comes from sub-departments of government which decide each year on their needs for the year that is to come. After allowing for present costs and future developments the experienced civil servant adds 10 per cent to the total, assuming (not always correctly) that his bid will be challenged at some stage by the financial branch. Assuming, however, that the expected wrangle takes place, the added 10 per cent is deleted at departmental level when the combined estimate comes to be drawn up. To this estimate the head of the department adds 10 per cent again, assuming (not always correctly) that his bid will be challenged by the Treasury. After the expected dispute, the revised estimate is laid before the responsible Minister, in Britain the Chancellor of the Exchequer, who consolidates all the departmental demands in a grand total and decides how the revenue can be made to equal the expenditure. With the agreement of his colleagues, he presents the nation with the bill. Here is the sum total of what the government needs, and these are the taxes which the people will have to pay.

But what, it will be asked, of the safeguards? Are not the accounts and estimates laid before the people's representatives? Is there no Treasury department to act as watchdog over the public purse? Are there no regulations framed to check extravagance and waste? All these safeguards undoubtedly exist. That they are futile is manifest from the known results. The reasons for their futility are less obvious, however, and are perhaps worth investigating, both as curious in themselves and as affording the clue to possible improvement. Briefly, the answer is that the accounts are meaningless, the Treasury ineffective, and the regulations so contrived as to make economy not so much difficult as impossible.

To deal first with the accounts and estimates presented to the House of Commons and available to the public, it is interesting to learn that a procedure of Exchequer receipts, dating from about 1129 and involving a Teller, a Tally Cutter, an Auditor, a Clerk of the Pells, a Scriptor Talliar, and several Chamberlains, survived until 1826. Apart from this, however, the basic fact to learn is that the accounts, such as they are, were designed for use during one particular period of history. Introduced during the Second Dutch War (in 1666), their primary object was to prevent money from the Navy Vote being spent by Charles II on the aptly entitled Duchess of Portsmouth. Even for this strictly limited purpose the method chosen met with no startling success. The system was revised, therefore, so as to assume its present form in 1689, from which year it more or less prevented William III from spending the money on *his* friends—who were not even girls.

Devised originally to guard the till, the public form of accounting dates from a period before book-keeping by

double entry was generally known except among noncon-
formists like Defoe. It dates, moreover, from an age when
few gentlemen knew even the arabic numerals, the clock
face in the stable yard showing only the roman figures
which the classically educated might be expected to understand. The result is that these public accounts, not of the
latest pattern even in 1689, are now beginning to verge on
the obsolete. They were revised, it is true, as a result of an
inquiry held in 1828–9, but the minority report of the
professional accountant was set aside in favour of the civil
servants' recommendations; these were against double entry
and left untouched the previous confusion between liabilities and assets, between capital and current. In 1904 Mr
Thomas Gibson Bowles, M.P., could therefore describe
the national accounts as 'unsystematic, unscientific, complicated, and so presented as to conceal and even to falsify
the facts.' In 1957 Mr John Appleby remarked that those

responsible for the public accounts seem to confuse themselves as well as everyone else.

It is fair to conclude, in short, that the British public accounts are not quite in line with current methods of accountancy. As a means of control, as a system of imparting information, they are scarcely worth the paper they are printed on. Accounts which would disgrace and discredit a third-rate dog-racing company are solemnly presented each year to the nation, and often presented by a businessman who ought to and does know better. So, far from being improved in form, these accounts have become more complex and muddled as the sums involved have proliferated and swollen. They are not true and they do not balance. It is the business of the accountant to give the facts of the financial position in the language of business, which is money. In that language he is to tell the truth and the whole truth. But those who present accounts to the nation do nothing of the kind. They present only a picture of archaic and dignified confusion.

And what of the Treasury, that guardian of the public weal? The accepted principle is that new expenditure is watched by the Treasury, old expenditure by the departments themselves. But what sort of a financial control is this? The division of responsibility is meaningless, for the problem of true economy is one and indivisible. Under such a system the extra clerk is demanded while the surplus clerk is retained. No office is ever declared redundant for fear that it should again be wanted and that its revival would mean a new approach to the Treasury. Nor would the surrender of an established post in department A make it any easier to establish a different post in department B, the two problems being considered in fact by separate authorities and as things totally unrelated to each other.

Such a practice can lead only to an irresponsible attitude among those forbidden to regard the problem as a whole. And experience suggests that grown men treated as children can behave in a very childish way.

As for the regulations imposed on the official, all they do is to add rigidity to waste. The whole system of appropriations is convenient only for cash accounting and useless for purposes of control. The departmental appropriation does not represent, to begin with, the cost of the department to which it relates. The Army Vote excludes stationery, for that is supplied by H.M. Stationery Office; the Stationery Office Vote excludes buildings (because these belong to the Office of Works) and so it goes on. Nor does the appropriation correspond to what is being done. Thus, the Navy's Votes are serialised from 1 (for pay) to 15 (for Additional Married Quarters), with separate Votes for such things as shipbuilding, armaments, and the Admiralty Office. Similarly, the Army Account is serialised into Votes, No. 1 for Pay, 7 for Supplies, 9 for Warlike Stores, and so forth. But neither the Navy nor the Army is organised like that. The Navy is organised into units afloat and ashore. The Army is organised into battalions, batteries, depots, and schools, for which individually no cost is shown. All that the system ensures is that money voted for vehicles should not be spent on weapons. But what if it were? And what is the point of the distinction? Parliament should not concern itself with that. What the faithful Commons might more usefully watch is the relative cost of administration and troops. How many extra battalions might be maintained for the sum spent on the finance branch of the War Office? Which are we more likely to need in an emergency— minute sheets or bayonets, ledgers or guns? That is a question of policy, whereas the total allocation for uniform clothing is almost solely a matter for the expert. The present rigidity is merely a waste of effort, money and time, serving no useful purpose of any kind.

So much for the official safeguards. In the light of their failure, all that remains to check extravagance is the press and the public. It might be thought that these would be effective, the press having no great love for bureaucracy and the body of taxpayers having a direct interest in the economical handling of their affairs. Why should press and public prove helpless where their own interests are so vitally concerned? The answer to that question is that true economy cannot be imposed on an organisation from outside; it must begin at the centre. From time to time the press does take up the cry of official extravagance, publishing details of apparent waste which the departments concerned are often in a position to contradict. More often the attacks are simply ignored, the civil servants well knowing that the newspapers will turn to something else in a few days' time. Suppose, however, that the outcry leads to questions in the House and that proof is forthcoming of some of the allegations made, what is the result? The inevitable sequel is the appointment of a Royal Commission, a device intended to postpone the business until after the next election. The official inquiry begins its laborious work, the members of the Commission being (let us assume) experienced, intelligent, energetic, and ruthless. They achieve little or nothing. Why? Because the whole process is basically wrong.

Let us suppose that naval dockyards are the subject of inquiry and that the Commission descends upon each in turn. The members include retired admirals and practising engineers who are far from ignorant of the matter in hand. They hear evidence. They ask searching questions: 'What are these fellows supposed to be doing?' 'What is all this junk?' 'How do you dispose of the clinker and wood shavings?' 'Why pay so many people to do so little?' But they soon observe a phenomenon which is best explained in terms of zoology. In the presence of wolves, sheep are said to form a tight bunch with horns outward and the weakest in the centre. Civil servants do the same. Faced by a common danger, they take up that formation, yielding nothing, denying everything, concealing all. This is a well-known fact of biology and one against which the commissioners must struggle in vain. Their report, when eventually printed, might just as well be placed in the toilet. Whatever happens to it, the matter is allowed to drop.

The ordinary taxpayer is often in a better position to know about waste in administration than either the politician or the journalist. For one thing, he may himself be employed in the dockyard. It is theoretically his interest as well as his duty to come forward and denounce extravagance when he sees it. He does nothing of the kind, and that for two distinct reasons. In the first place he stands to gain nothing but unpopularity and abuse, being likely to be regarded as at best a crank, at worst a spy. In the second place, he knows perfectly well that the money saved in one direction will certainly be wasted in another. Nothing he can do will reduce the tax he has to pay. So he wisely decides to say nothing and keep the good opinion of his neighbours. In matters of public expenditure no help is to be expected from the public at large unless the informant is personally rewarded and at the same time assured that all savings made will go to the reduction of the taxes to which he is subject.

To summarise the position, the public revenue is regarded as limitless and expenditure rises eternally to meet it, and the various devices which are supposed to check expenditure fail to do so, being wrongly conceived and imperfectly motivated. The problem is a serious one and would seem to merit our attention. What is to be done? The modern instinct is to frame new regulations and laws, of which there are already more than enough. The better plan, less fashionable today, is to re-motivate the people actually concerned, penalising the extravagance we now reward and rewarding the economy we now penalise. As a first step towards redirecting the flood, we need to reverse the whole process of government finance. Ministers should not begin by ascertaining what the departments need. They should begin by asking what the country can afford to spend. We do not base our personal budget on what our past extravagances have taught us to like but on the income we can fairly expect to receive. We do not, in short, plan to spend what we have not got. The same principle should apply to public as it does to individual finance. The first question to decide is the ratio between the revenue and the gross national product. What proportion of the national income should the government demand? What proportion of the individual's income can the government safely take? And what happens when that proportion is exceeded? Economists (with one notable exception) have fought shy of this problem, allowing it to be assumed that, where government expenditure is concerned, the sky is the limit. It is one aim of this chapter to suggest that there are other and lower limits; a limit beyond which taxation is undesirable, a limit beyond which it is dangerous and a limit (finally) beyond which it is fatal. And these limits are clearly indicated by both economic theory and historical fact.

GOVERNMENT

In the light of these known dangers, it is for the Cabinet to decide upon the ratio between government expenditure and gross national product. That decision taken, there is a total fixed for the revenue, a total within which the Ministries have to work. It is for the Cabinet again to decide upon the distribution of this total between the departments. To individual ministers would fall the responsibility of subdividing departmental allocations between the various branches and units. No department under this system would be asked to submit an estimate. It would be told, instead, to keep within a total. All that would concern the House of Commons would be the gross expenditure and its allocation to Ministries. Members of Parliament need not be asked to vote on the relative amounts to be spent on petrol and grease, floor polish and boots. They *can* fairly compare the value for money given by the Air Force or the British Council, by Education or by Health. For purposes of control, they need no more than that by way of forecast, together with *real* accounts of expenditure in the past—such accounts as they have never yet been allowed to see.

The obvious advantage of the system here described is that a limit is placed on expenditure. An advantage as important, if less obvious, is that the expenditure becomes flexible within each Ministry, department, sub-department, and unit. The officials themselves are thus made responsible for economy, their success or failure becoming instantly apparent from the accounts of the following year. It is the executive officers, and they alone, who know where economies can safely be made. Once they understand that the development they want in one direction is conditional on their economising in another direction, the rest can safely be left to them; provided that promotion goes first to the man who shows where the money can be saved. Yet another advantage, still less obvious at first sight, would be the elimination of Treasury supervision with all its evils of divided control, inefficiency, and waste. In place of distrustful interference, the public official would know only the strong leash of account and audit. He would be compelled to accept responsibility, free to display initiative, and forced to recognise that cost and value are but different aspects of the same idea.

Once the decision has been made to approach the financial problem from the right direction, it would remain only to enlist public aid in the prevention of waste. For this purpose the first need is for an independent tribunal to which all proposals for saving money could be submitted; a body of, say, three, to include a government representative (the Steward, perhaps, of the Chiltern Hundreds). This tribunal would hear representations from the public and from the departments affected and would decide finally whether each suggested economy were feasible or not. Each decision in favour of an economy would lead to a ministerial order to the department concerned, reducing its future allocation by the amount to be saved. It would be the further function of the tribunal to reward each successful applicant by the remission of his income tax to a total related in some way to the amount of the saving. There should also be provision to ensure that all sums saved should go, not to another department, nor to the Treasury, but solely to the reduction of the National Debt. The last function of the tribunal would be to recommend for honours the citizens whose suggestions had resulted in the greatest economies, as also the civil servants who had been most successful in reducing needless expenditure. A minor revolution would date from the day when officials came to realise that a knighthood is more readily to be won by saving money than by spending it.

It is not to be supposed that the reform of the national finances would be unopposed. In this field of administration the reformer will be faced, inevitably, by a closed phalanx of civil servants representing one of the strongest vested interests in the world. Their opposition, though passive, will be formidable. To all proposals for a proper system of accounts they will reply with a pitying smile that it was tried once at the War Office, found wasteful and long ago abandoned. They will then retire behind a smoke screen of technical mysteries, muttering finally that public finance is a more complex matter than is generally realised. Figures cannot lie but liars can figure.

The hieratic and esoteric attitudes observable in the Treasury have led to the creation of a special term to describe their cult: esoterrorism. Its devotees are the esoterrorists of Whitehall. In the 18th century these same people concealed the mysteries of the Exchequer in medieval Latin and in the court hand which the law courts abandoned in 1733, continuing to do so until the Exchequer itself (but not its Chancellor) was abolished in the reign of William IV. Nor was the Exchequer alone in its archaic confusion, for an investigation of 1570 into the London Customs broke down completely because 'the officers have used such an obscure way in keeping of their books.' A Member of Parliament exclaimed in 1961, 'I stand amazed that in the best times and Governments, things should be in such darkness.' The special commissioners of 1829 reported that 'The Annual Accounts leave millions unexplained and unaccounted for in detail'—which was found again to be the case in 1844 and is still so today. The darkness has become, if anything, darker still,

41

for to the original confusion of the accounts has been added the babble of consultants and the jargon of the London School of Economics. From being merely a nuisance, esoterrorism is fast becoming a religion.

The strongholds of esoterrorism have been impregnable since the days of Gladstone. Amid the entanglements which surround their position are the graves of their former assailants, Florence Nightingale, Sir John Keane, and Lord Randolph Churchill. There too is the mutilated tombstone of Sir Charles Harris, the man who nearly betrayed the whole position, on the anniversary of whose death the leading esoterrorists still exchange a barbed wire. Let no one imagine that this citadel will yield to the first assault. Let no one doubt, however, that it will yield to the last.

FINANCE

4

Law of Triviality or Point of Vanishing Interest

PEOPLE WHO UNDERSTAND HIGH FINANCE ARE OF TWO kinds: those who have vast fortunes of their own and those who have nothing at all. To the actual millionaire a million pounds is something real and comprehensible. To the applied mathematician and the lecturer in economics (assuming both to be practically starving) a million pounds is at least as real as a thousand, they having never possessed either sum. But the world is full of people who fall between these two categories, knowing nothing of millions but well accustomed to think in thousands, and it is of these that finance committees are mostly comprised. The result is a phenomenon that has often been observed but never yet investigated. It might be termed the Law of Triviality. Briefly stated, it means that the time spent on any item of the agenda will be in inverse proportion to the sum involved.

On second thoughts, the statement that this law has

never been investigated is not entirely accurate. Some
work has actually been done in this field, but the investigators pursued a line of inquiry that led them nowhere. They
assumed that the greatest significance should attach to the
order in which items of the agenda are taken. They assumed, further, that most of the available time will be
spent on items one to seven and that the later items will be
allowed automatically to pass. The result is well known.
The derision with which Dr Guggenheim's lecture was
received at the Muttworth Conference may have been thought
excessive at the time, but all further discussions on this
topic have tended to show that his critics were right. Years
had been wasted in a research of which the basic assump-
tions were wrong. We realise now that position on the
agenda is a minor consideration, so far, at least, as
this problem is concerned. We consider also that Dr
Guggenheim was lucky to escape, as he did, in his underwear. Had he dared to put his lame conclusions before the
later conference in September, he would have faced something more than derision. The view would have been taken
that he was deliberately wasting time.

If we are to make further progress in this investigation we
must ignore all that has so far been done. We must start at
the beginning and understand fully the way in which a
finance committee actually works. For the sake of the
general reader this can be put in dramatic form thus:

Chairman: 'We come now to Item Nine. Our Treasurer,
Mr McPhail, will report.'

Mr McPhail: 'The estimate for the Atomic Reactor is
before you, sir, set forth in Appendix H of the subcommit-
tee's report. You will see that the general design and
layout has been approved by Professor McFission. The

total cost will amount to £10,000,000. The contractors, Messrs McNab and McHash, consider that the work should be completed by April 1963. Mr McFee, the consulting engineer, warns us that we should not count on completion before October, at the earliest. In this view he is supported by Dr McHeap, the well-known geophysicst, who refers to the probable need for piling at the lower end of the site. The plan of the main building is before you—see Appendix IX—and the blueprint is laid on the table. I shall be glad to give any further information that members of this committee may require.'

Chairman: 'Thank you, Mr McPhail, for your very lucid explanation of the plan as proposed. I will now invite the members present to give us their views.'

It is necessary to pause at this point and consider what views the members are likely to have. Let us suppose that they number eleven, including the Chairman but excluding the Secretary. Of these eleven members, four—including the Chairman—do not know what a reactor is. Of the remainder, three do not know what it is for. Of those who know its purpose, only two have the least idea of what it should cost. One of these is Mr Isaacson, the other is Mr Brickworth. Either is in a position to say something. We may suppose that Mr Isaacson is the first to speak.

Mr Isaacson: 'Well, Mr Chairman, I could wish that I felt more confidence in our contractors and consultant. Had we gone to Professor Levi in the first instance, and had the contract been given to Messrs David and Goliath, I should have been happier about the whole scheme. Mr Lyon-Daniels would not have wasted our time with wild guesses about the possible delay in completion, and Dr

47

Moses Bullrush would have told us definitely whether piling would be wanted or not.'

Chairman: 'I am sure we all appreciate Mr Isaacson's anxiety to complete this work in the best possible way. I feel, however, that it is rather late in the day to call in new technical advisers. I admit that the main contract has still to be signed, but we have already spent very large sums. If we reject the advice for which we have paid, we shall have to pay as much again.'

(*Other members murmur agreement.*)

Mr Isaacson: 'I should like my observation to be minuted.'

Chairman: 'Certainly. Perhaps Mr Brickworth also has something to say on this matter?'

Now Mr Brickworth is almost the only man there who knows what he is talking about. There is a great deal he could say. He distrusts that round figure of £10,000,000. Why should it come out to exactly that? Why need they demolish the old building to make room for the new approach? And who is McHeap, anyway? Is he the man who was sued last year by the Trickle and Driedup Oil Corporation? But Brickworth does not know where to begin. The other members could not read the blueprint if he referred to it. He would have to begin by explaining what a reactor is and no one there would admit that he did not already know. Better to say nothing.

Mr Brickworth: 'I have no comment to make.'

Chairman: 'Does any other member wish to speak? Very well. I may take it then that the plans and estimates are approved? Thank you. May I now sign the main contract on your behalf? (*Murmur of agreement.*) Thank you. We can now move on to Item Ten.'

Allowing a few seconds for rustling papers and unrolling diagrams, the time spent on Item Nine will have been just two minutes and a half. The meeting is going well. But some members feel uneasy about Item Nine. They wonder inwardly whether they have really been pulling their weight. It is too late to query that reactor scheme, but they would like to demonstrate, before the meeting ends, that they are alive to all that is going on.

Chairman: 'Item Ten. Bicycle shed for the use of the clerical staff. An estimate has been received from Messrs Bodger and Woodworm, who undertake to complete the work for the sum of £350. Plans and specifications are before you, gentlemen.'

Mr Softleigh: 'Surely, Mr Chairman, this sum is excessive, I note that the roof is to be of aluminum. Would not asbestos be cheaper?

Mr Holdfast: 'I agree with Mr Softleigh about the cost, but the roof should, in my opinion, be of galvanised iron. I am inclined to think that the shed could be built for £300, or even less.'

Mr Daring: 'I would go further, Mr Chairman. I question whether this shed is really necessary. We do too much for our staff as it is. They are never satisfied, that is the trouble. They will be wanting garages next.'

Mr Holdfast: 'No, I can't support Mr Daring on this occasion. I think that the shed is needed. It is a question of material and cost . . .'

The debate is fairly launched. A sum of £350 is well within everybody's comprehension. Everyone can visualise a bicycle shed. Discussion goes on, therefore, for forty-five minutes, with the possible result of saving some £50. Members at length sit back with a feeling of achievement.

Chairman: 'Item Eleven. Refreshments supplied at meetings of the Joint Welfare Committee. Monthly, £2.'

Mr Softleigh: 'What type of refreshment is supplied on these occasions?'

Chairman: 'Coffee, I understand.'

Mr Holdfast: 'And this means an annual charge of—let me see—£24?'

Chairman: 'That is so.'

Mr Daring: 'Well, really, Mr Chairman. I question whether this is justified. How long do these meetings last?'

Now begins an even more acrimonious debate. There may be members of the committee who might fail to distinguish between asbestos and galvanised iron, but every man there knows about coffee—what it is, how it should be made, where it should be bought—and whether indeed it should be bought at all. This item on the agenda will occupy the members for an hour and a quarter, and they will end by asking the Secretary to procure further information, leaving the matter to be decided at the next meeting.

It would be natural to ask at this point whether a still smaller sum—£10, perhaps, or £5—would occupy the Finance Committee for a proportionately longer time. On this point, it must be admitted, we are still ignorant. Our tentative conclusion must be that there is a point at which the whole tendency is reversed, the committee members concluding that the sum is beneath their notice. Research has still to establish the point at which this reversal occurs. The transition from the £24 debate (an hour and a quarter) to the £10,000,000 debate (two and a half minutes) is indeed an abrupt one. It would be the more interesting to establish the exact point at which it occurs. More than that, it would be of practical value. Supposing, for example, that the point of vanishing interest is represented by the sum of £15, the Treasurer with an item of £26 on the agenda might well decide to present it as two items, one of £14 and the other of £12, with an evident saving in time and effort.

Conclusions at this juncture can be merely tentative, but

there is some reason to suppose that the point of vanishing interest represents the sum the individual committee member is willing to lose on a bet or subscribe to a charity. An inquiry on these lines conducted on racecourses and in Methodist chapels, might go far toward solving the problem. Far greater difficulty may be encountered in attempting to discover the exact point at which the sum involved becomes too large to discuss at all. One thing apparent, however, is that the time spent on £10,000,000 and on £10 may well prove to be the same. The present estimated time of two and a half minutes is by no means exact, but there is clearly a space of time—something between two and four and a half minutes—which suffices equally for the largest and the smallest sums.

Much further investigation remains to be done, but the final results, when published, cannot fail to be of absorbing interest and of immediate value to mankind.

5

Limits of Taxation or Self-Defeat

TAXES CAN BE GROUPED INTO TWO BROAD CATEGORIES: those we impose on ourselves and those we inflict upon other people. Taxes in the first category, examples of which in history are extremely rare, are self-limiting. They may rise in a time of emergency but, once the crisis is past, they should tend to fall. The United States in their earlier days offered an example of taxation falling within this category. Nineteenth-century Britain offered another such example, at least for a time, and other instances are known in both the ancient and modern periods of history. On the other hand, most taxes clearly come within the category of burdens imposed by some people upon others. The taxes decreed by ancient monarchies were all of this type and so are the graduated taxes of today at all levels above the average, being voted by those to whom the heaviest rates will not apply.

The taxes inflicted by some people upon others will

inevitably rise as expenditure rises, and expenditure will rise in accordance with Parkinson's Second Law. Their only limit is at the point where the victim refuses to pay, and to that point they will rise by the principle which governs their growth. In ancient times that point of refusal was reached when the tax demand rose much above 10 per cent of the gross product. Our information is admittedly meagre, but such figures as we possess range between 5 and 10 per cent in cases where the entire economy is known to have collapsed. Now it is obvious that the amount of the tax will be something a little above the cost of its avoidance. For a customs duty 2½ per cent was originally the natural limit, and about 10 per cent for a tax on land. That level must have been related to the cost and the risk of migrating elsewhere. An early example of such a migration is to be found in the Book of Exodus. Pharaoh taxed the Israelites in terms of service: 'And the Egyptians made the children of Israel to serve with rigour: and they made their lives bitter with hard bondage, in mortar, and in brick, and in all manner of service in the field.' At some point unspecified in this raising of the assessment, the Israelites judged that the time had come to go elsewhere. In 19th-century Malaya the Chinese tin miners would yield a Malay chief up to 10 per cent of their output as payment for 'protection.' If he asked more they drifted to another mining area where the chief asked less. Some chiefs reacted to this very much as Pharaoh did and with about as much result. As a reckless generalisation we can say that the productive people of the world have discovered from experience that they will always have to yield 10 per cent to somebody, whether to a gangster, a feudal lord, or a department of Inland Revenue. It comes to much the same thing in any case. To escape from one tax gatherer will usually mean paying blackmail to another. Up to about 10 per cent the exaction is in accordance, it would seem, with a law of nature. When it rises much above that level, the time has come for the Israelites to study the atlas. There may be better places than Egypt; and in point of fact there are.

In studying the history of public finance the temptation is to conclude that people are willing to pay taxes up to a certain point; up to 10 per cent for example. This would be an entirely mistaken idea. Normal people are reluctant to pay any tax of any proportion at any time. Their grievance will be just as vocal whether the taxes are heavy or light. The Chinese never regarded payment of a tenth as 'perfectly just and equitable' whatever any scholar may say to the contrary. But they did regard such a tax as inevitable and customary. Now, in noting the resignation of ancient

taxpayers, we should also note the circumstances which limited their liability. For, under the empires of Rome and China, migration at least between provinces was relatively easy. The situation is entirely different when there is nowhere to go or when taxation elsewhere is just as bad. In these radically altered circumstances the barrier at 10 per cent is removed and taxes will rise to a new maximum. Within the rigid frontiers of modern nationalism, for example, the taxpayer is indeed captive. His taxes will rise, therefore, until they reach a new point of refusal. At what level is this point to be found?

This important question was discussed by that able Victorian economist, J. R. McCulloch, who wrote as follows:

> Oppression, it has been said, either raises men into heroes or sinks them into slaves; and taxation, according to its magnitude and the mode in which it is imposed, either makes men industrious, enterprising and wealthy, or indolent, dispirited and impoverished.

McCulloch here judges the limit of taxable capacity by the reaction of the taxpayers, which might obviously vary with other circumstances. It is clear, however, from his subsequent remarks, that he was contemplating taxes within a certain range. He thus expected to find great resistance to a direct tax amounting to between 10 and 15 per cent of the taxpayer's income—such resistance indeed as to make it a tax on honesty and a bounty on fraud:

> . . . were it carried to any great height, or to 10, 15 or 20 per cent, it could generate the most barefaced prostitution of principle, and do much to sap that nice sense of honour which is the only sure foundation of national probity and virtue.

McCulloch's conclusion on this subject was more than borne out by experience. The reaction of the taxpayer who cannot escape the tax by migration is to reduce it by some other form of avoidance. We may read that British taxpayers of 1909 were thought thus to have reduced their theoretical tax of 1s. to 7¾d. in the pound. Above 10 per cent the effort to avoid the tax is intensified, as the time and trouble spent yields a better return than would the effort to have made additional income, itself again subject to the tax. It is clear that a direct tax of from 10 to 20 per cent of the taxpayer's income tends to deflect initiative and ingenuity into a new channel and one quite profitless to the community as a whole. More than that, the brains devoted to tax avoidance have to be matched by the brains devoted to tax collection. And, despite all the official ingenuity displayed, each tax increase yields a poorer result than the last. The point might be reached, at least in theory, when no further tax increase would improve the revenue. Before that point is reached, however, the situation would have been transformed in another way.

What happens when direct taxation takes as much as 25 per cent of the national income was first noticed by Lord Keynes in about 1923. It was he who pointed out that taxation, beyond a certain point, is the cause of inflation. When there is a high tax on the profits of industry, employers can reduce the tax by distributing the profits among their staff; a form of generosity which costs little. With this lessened resistance to wage demands, the value of the currency declines. One way in which profits can be distributed is through entertainment. Some American observers have already called attention to the inflationary effect of the 'expense account economy.' Many minor executives prefer a generous expense account to a raise in salary which would be heavily taxed and more soberly spent. It is they who support the so-called 'expense account restaurants,' places of exotic décor where patrons lunch in a darkness which is all but complete. They cannot see to read the prices on the menu but these, in the special circumstances, are irrelevant. For the company, it is a less expensive form of remuneration. For the community it is yet another, if minor, cause of inflation. As inflation progresses, a policy of devaluation then finds general support, with the result that the State's creditors, the investors in government stock, are cheated in what has become the normal fashion. Writing off a proportion of the national debt, the State becomes solvent again and the real value of the taxes will begin to fall. The argument, as put forward by Colin Clark in 1945, is that taxation exceeding 25 per cent of the national income must defeat its own purpose. This argument attracted considerable notice at the time but was not generally agreed among economists. While many experts admitted that some sort of limit must exist, they considered that this could vary according to national character and other circumstances. Sir Stafford Cripps is known to have believed that the British would bear almost limitless taxation, and this is clearly the assumption that has coloured British fiscal policy. And those who share Cripps' belief can point to the British record since 1939. The tax collectors of Britain (central and local), who took 25.4 per cent of the national income in 1938 and 39.8 per cent in 1947, were actually taking a larger share (40.1 per cent) in 1950 and no economic catastrophe had ensued. The whole subject was discussed at the 1953 Symposium of the Tax Institute, most delegates to which more or less agreed that Britian was taxing itself to death. Few, however, were prepared to say at what point rising taxation should have been checked, and fewer still would have agreed on a rule applicable to all countries at all periods of history.

One thing apparent from all discussions on this subject is that people will pay heavy taxes when fighting for their existence. When the alternative appears to be national destruction, taxes of up to 50 per cent of the national income may well be paid without much complaint. The point of refusal is reached only when the doubt arises as to whether existence is worth while. It is also apparent that the atmosphere of crisis can be retained to some extent after the war is over. Appeals to patriotism can still be made, with promises of a better world to come. There is no particular reason for supposing that an orgy of mutual destruction should result in a better world, but the promise is often made and often believed. In Britain at least, taxes amounting to 40 per cent of the national income have been paid without protest for a number of years. The temptation among those responsible is to assume that all is well and that comparable taxes can be borne indefinitely. In fact, however, the results of oppressive taxation are cumulative and slow. Historical examples serve to illustrate a strangling process spread over many years. Today the tempo is quickened but not so much as to be readily perceptible. It is the more important, therefore, to note the symptoms which mark the progress of the disease. They represent the loss, successively, of influence, freedom, and stability.

Loss of influence follows from loss of strength. Among some of the potential belligerents of 1909 the figures for total taxation were as follows:

	Population to nearest 1,000	*Taxation*
		£
United Kingdom	45,469,000	151,955,000
France	39,252,000	111,686,082
Austria-Hungary	51,251,000	95,055,544
United States	88,926,000	109,384,916
Germany	63,879,000	88,055,333
Russia	160,095,000	72,853,500
Italy	34,270,000	50,577,962
Japan	53,273,000	32,831,510

Between these countries there were significant differences in development and wealth. The fact remains, however, that Britain was the country most heavily taxed in the years before World War I, with France a bad second and Austria-Hungary a good third. These were the countries whose influence declined sharply in the years which followed the war. The two countries where taxation was lowest were those whose influence increased the most. By 1938 the most heavily taxed countries were, in the following order, Germany, Britain, and France: again the countries whose influence was afterwards to decline. While other factors must have their importance, a country like the United States, which in 1938 combined wealth with a low rate of taxation, was obviously more formidable than a country which was heavily taxed before the war even began. The contrast between high taxable capacity and low taxes is a sign of latent strength and one not wasted on the world at large. Nor will rival powers fail to notice the high level of taxation maintained today in countries like Britain and France. Neither country, they conclude, will ever fight again except in defending its frontiers. A country so placed, with no visible margin of strength, can have only a dwindling influence in international affairs. That such a toothless country will do anything to extend or even secure its wider interests is believed by nobody. It can do little even to maintain the peace. For most purposes it can be simply ignored.

The first effect, then, of a high rate of peacetime taxation is to reduce a country's influence in world affairs. The second effect is to be measured in the loss of individual freedom. On this subject the words of Thomas Jefferson cannot be quoted too often:

> I place economy among the first and most important virtues, and public debt as the greatest of dangers to be feared. . . . To preserve our independence, we must not let our rulers load us with public debt. . . . We must make our choice between economy and liberty or profusion and servitude.

> . . . If we run into such debts, we must be taxed in our meat and drink, in our necessities and comforts, in our labor and in our amusements. . . . If we can prevent the Government from wasting the labor of the people, under the pretense of caring for them, they will be happy.

These are prophetic words. Wasting the labour of the people 'under the pretense of caring for them' is exactly what our governments do. Freedom is founded upon ownership of property. It involves self-expression in terms of architecture and art. It cannot exist where the rulers own everything, nor even when they concede some limited right of tenure. But the modern belief is that spendable income is a concession of the State. The taxation which is intended to promote equality, the taxation which exceeds the real public need, and above all the tax which is so graduated as to prevent the accumulation of private capital, is inconsistent with freedom. Against a State which owns everything, the individual has neither the means of defence nor anything to defend. For the normal human being who is not a creative artist or scientist by profession the means of self-expression consist largely of rooms to modify and gardens to tend, trees to plant and offspring to rear. Losing these opportunities for expression, the individual loses individuality, freedom, and hope.

The third effect of a high rate of peacetime taxation is the loss of stability. There are many human achievements, including some of the finest, which need more than a single lifetime for completion. The individual can compose a symphony or paint a canvas, build up a business or restore order in a city. He cannot build a cathedral or grow an avenue of oak trees. Still less can he gain the stature essential to statesmanship in a highly developed and complex society. There is a need for continuity of effort, spread over several generations, and for just such a continuity as governments must lack. Given the party system more especially, under the democratic form of rule, policy is continually modified or reversed. A family can be biologically stable in a way that a modern legislature is not. It is to families, therefore, that we look for such stability as society may need. But how can the family function if subject to crippling taxes during every lifetime and partial confiscation with every death? How can one generation provide the springboard for the next? Without such a springboard, all must start alike, and none can excel; and where none can excel nothing excellent will result. Without sustained effort, without stability, no civilisation can for long survive.

From this analysis it may not seem easy to fix on a certain level of taxation as representing the maximum. So far it would seem that there are successive points at which evil results successively appear. With peacetime taxation amounting to over 10 per cent of the national income, capital will begin to migrate. If its flight is prevented, whether by circumstances or by legislation, taxes can rise to 20 per cent but against a stiffening opposition which takes the form of tax avoidance and evasion carried to the utmost lengths of determination and skill. Above 20 per cent each tax increase will produce proportionately less. Above 25 per cent there is serious inflation, reducing the value of the revenue collected. Above 30 per cent the decline in national influence, observable long before to the expert, becomes obvious to the world at large. At 35 per cent there is a visible decline in freedom and stability. At 36 per cent there is disaster, complete and final, although not always immediate. Taxation beyond that point, feasible and perhaps necessary in time of war, is lethal in time of peace. Of the taxation precipice, 36 per cent (for most countries) represents the brink.

In one respect the simile of the precipice is misleading, for the fall of a nation is less dramatic than the fall of a single vehicle or man. It can live for a time on borrowings and capital. There will be a dwindling but still valuable stock of integrity, enterprise, energy, and hope. Older people will go on working from habit even after the younger folk have seen that it is pointless. People will go on saving from habit even after they have seen past savings shrivel to nothing. People will retain a professional pride for years after they have ceased to retain more than a fraction of their professional fee. The machine goes on for a while even after the power has been switched off. For a time the slowing down is not even perceptible. Then the whine of the engine becomes a throb, the throb becomes a slow pulsation and that becomes in turn a measured and lessening groan and hiss. The blurred flywheel becomes visible, its spokes marking a slower rhythm, and so the engine wheezes and grunts its way to a final grinding, clanging halt. It is the end of the journey and, in this instance, the end of the train.

From this necessarily simplified account of what may be expected to happen there emerges as yet no single, clear rule as to what the ideal rate of taxation ought to be. Nor is the situation made simpler by the fact that some services— education, health and life insurance—would have to be provided by the individual if they were not provided by the state. The extent of these services makes it difficult, even, to compare the weight of taxation as between one country and another. What is clear, however, is that the progressive transference of responsibility from the individual to the State cannot but weaken individuality itself. There is clearly, somewhere, a line to be drawn. The traditional 10 per cent has the support of experience but there may be special reasons for exceeding it. Where these reasons exist, taxation should stop at the point where it absorbs 20 per cent of the national income provided that it is strictly proportionate and that no income suffers direct taxation beyond the limit of 25 per cent. Countries which have recently exceeded the bounds of safety are (in order of extravagance) the United Kingdom, France, New Zealand, Japan, and the United States. Some of these may yet struggle back to a position of financial stability. Time is short, however, and the effort is long overdue. The problem is not initially how to reduce expenditure on social services or defence. The problem is how, first of all, to redirect into useful channels all the effort and ingenuity now being spent, on the one hand, in the collection, on the other hand, in the avoidance, of tax.

6

Avoidance of Tax
or The Cheshire Cat

ANY SCRUTINY OF THE HISTORY OF TAXATION MUST leave the student with a sense of wonder that civilisation should have survived at all. That nations have retained or recovered a measure of prosperity is certainly a matter for surprise. It must be remembered, however, that the effects of overtaxation were not immediate in the historical examples already cited. Empires or countries strangled by their own revenue departments do not necessarily collapse at once. The process may take time and is not at first perceptible. Many an industrial or commercial business will drift on for fifty years after its initial momentum has been lost. States do the same, living on their past reputation and spending their capital reserves. Time is needed to produce a new generation, one which has been accustomed from childhood to the sense of failure. More time is needed to allow this new generation to gain high office. Even then the memory will linger for a while of past enterprise that was not merely legal but honourable, of past endeavours which ended not with fiscal penalty but with public recognition. Men will look to the future even after the future has been mortgaged. To deprive them of hope takes time.

But long before that stage the combined effect of income tax and death duty should have reduced society to a dull level of financial mediocrity. Almost everyone in Britain and the United States should be living in a small suburban house with a small suburban garden, drawing a small suburban income and supporting a small suburban wife. Of parts of Australia this could almost be said to be true, and there are other countries in which this pattern of life is increasingly familiar. But there are reasons for supposing that, elsewhere, the theory still differs from the fact. Rolls-Royces and Bentleys still effortlessly overtake the other cars on the road. People still send their sons to Eton or Exeter, Groton, or Rugby. At the most extravagant resorts the beaches are far from deserted; and the blue waters of the Mediterranean still reflect the sails of some quite expensive yachts. The days of financial privilege may be passing but they clearly have not passed.

Contemplation of this spectacle has produced in England the people who have come to be described as angry young men, persons whose anger may well outlast their youth. They would seem to represent a class of people whose school and university education, provided at state expense, has prepared them only for frustration. On the one hand, the Labour Party has no use for its own intellectuals, least of all those for whose education some Co-operative Society has actually paid. On the other, the doors of privilege are still firmly closed against the products of Wiggleworth and Redbrick. Assured in youth that the peerage is being taxed out of existence and that the Etonian has no place in democratic society, these Redbrick graduates find that it is they themselves who have no place. Their frustration assumes literary form and they speak bitterly of the 'tax dodgers' whose continued prosperity is at once mysterious and unwelcome.

Those who speak sardonically about 'tax dodgers' reveal only their ignorance of the entire subject. Taxes cannot be dodged. They can be either avoided or evaded, depending upon whether the method used is legal or otherwise. Both methods are as old as taxation itself, as we have seen, and tax consultants were engaged in their 'laborious and intricate work' at least as early as 1852. On the subject of tax evasion a book could be written, but this is not it. Nor is it likely that a volume on that topic would be as useful as it might be voluminous. When we see booklets on 'How to write a best-selling novel' we conclude that their authors, if they really know what they profess to teach, should be

writing novels, not booklets on authorship. In the same way, an author really skilled in tax evasion would find the practice more profitable than any public explanation of the theory. So there are reasons for doubting whether a useful book on tax evasion is ever likely to appear on the bookstalls. It is even a question whether a book on how to break the law might not itself be illegal.

There can be no suspicion of illegality about a book (still less, a mere chapter) on tax avoidance, but its inherent limitations must be understood. The man who has found a loophole in the law, one through which he can drive his gold-plated Cadillac, will certainly keep the secret to himself. For an individual to use the method in question may be unremarked or unopposed, but the spectacle of a whole herd converging on the same gap in the fence would invite remedial legislation, passed with a speed observable in no other kind of parliamentary activity. In such a chapter as this, then, the reader can expect no more than a discussion of principles, a show of historical erudition and some allusion to avoidance methods for which there would seem to be no legislative remedy.

First of all, it must be understood that the basic method of tax avoidance is today, as it has been from the beginning, to leave the country. Wealthy and distinguished men of British origin are thus to be found in Jersey, Tangier, Kenya, Bermuda, Tahiti, or the Seychelles. Places of refuge for the taxpayer are territories where the tax burden is significantly less, where opportunities exist for investment or earning, and which possess a suitable agreement with Britain for the avoidance of double-taxation. Territories fulfilling these basic conditions are relatively few, and of these few the majority, perhaps, have drawbacks of their own such as earthquakes, communists, cockroaches, colonial officials, centipedes, fevers, sociologists, and snakes. Even the most apparently idyllic island can become the target for missionary activity or ballistic missiles. Nevertheless, this simple method of tax avoidance is open to all at the price of exile, and open to companies as well as to individuals. Much of what would have been the British merchant marine sails now under Greek ownership and flies the brave, battle-torn ensign of Liberia or of Panama.

For those whose business or interests, tastes or health compel them to stay in Manchester, Wellington, or Montreal, the problem is not as simple. It would not be too much to say that the tax situation is apt to be complex, uncertain, obscure, and confused. Amidst the obscurities there looms, however, one fundamental principle, and that is the distinction between capital and income. In the department concerned with tax collection—but in no other public department—this distinction is generally recognised. It is recognised for the reason that income is subject to tax and capital subject to death duties. It is therefore the object of the tax avoider to have no income (but merely capital) while he lives, no capital (but merely income) when he dies. The tax collector's point of view is exactly the opposite. He sees nothing but income during the victim's life and nothing but capital at his death. To reconcile these diametrically opposite views within the strained and tottering framework of the law is definitely a task for the expert. The conflict is hedged about by technicalities, the law turning out to be vague and the lawyers vaguer still. Massed formidably on the one side is the artillery of the statutes, thunderous in sound and fury but haphazard in direction. In ambush on the other side are past verdicts of the courts, almost inaudible but carefully aimed. To pass even relatively unscathed through this combined barrage and fusillade is difficult for anyone and impossible for most.

One fact apparent at the outset is that capital is more easily preserved than income. That is why the ranks of the English aristocracy have become more exclusive, perhaps, than ever before. To found a county family, complete with estates and castle, peerage and park, is now virtually impracticable. To retain the inherited position may not be easy, but it now means the maintenance of what no one else can ever have again. The social value of nobility is therefore increasing, to the annoyance of the angry young men, and even the great house is nowadays less of a burden and more of an asset. The old families are unassailably situated as compared with the new. In much the same way, age generally is in a stronger position than youth. The older directors and surgeons, authors and managers, dramatists and artists mostly enjoy the advantage of having made money before 1939; or even, in some instances, before 1909. They had made their capital before taxation became ruinous. All the younger men are penalised, by contrast, for being born too late in the century.

For people with capital to preserve, the problem is not insoluble. Their first precaution must be to give everything away to their heirs by deed of gift, contriving to live thereafter for a minimum period of five years. The chief objection to this policy derives from the difficulty of knowing when the death is likely to occur. The impatient heir might see this transaction taking place when his father reaches the age of fifty-five, while the father (with whom the decision lies) might think it premature to take such a drastic step before reaching his seventieth birthday. When such a father dies at the age of seventy-four, as seems inevitable, his son and heir is all too apt to burst a blood vessel, thus incurring a second load of death duties before the first has ever been assessed. Those who visit the stately homes of England are often told that the Duke is bedridden or that the Marquess's bath-chair may be glimpsed on the distant terrace. They are correct in concluding, as they always do, that the Marquess died some time ago, that the bath-chair contains a dummy figure and that the nobleman's body has been placed in the Frigidaire (family model) until such time as the death can be safely announced. While there may be little danger of the secret being revealed, the inconveniences involved in this type of estate-duty avoidance are all too obvious. For one thing, the refrigerator may be wanted for something else. It is for this reason that many people prefer the alternative method of vesting the whole property in a privately owned company, which will not die.

For people with capital, there are also ways of apparently foregoing income. They all work on the principle that what might, at first glance, appear to be income is really only an appreciation of capital. A method once popular was to buy and sell shares in such a way as to avoid receiving a dividend. As most shares rise in value before the dividend falls due, being marked down again after it has been paid, the tax avoider has had good reason to sell them before the payment and buy them back afterwards. This practice has been discouraged somewhat by a tax levied on the transference of shares, as a result of which it became necessary to do rather more than buy and sell the same stock. With reasonably good advice, however, the handling of investments is not really difficult. Many types of property have been rising in value for years, city real estate being a case in point. Great gains involve appreciable risks but a steady and inconspicuous capital appreciation is fairly easy to arrange.

While taxable unearned income can thus be minimised it is usually unwise to deny having any income at all. Income there must be, but kept under rigid control by the formation, or (even better) the acquisition of a limited liability company. A company formed for purposes of tax avoidance is usually agricultural in character and associated with some singularly unproductive acreage of land. Such profits as may arise from the other activities of the company are offset by losses on the farm. These losses arise in two ways. In the first place, it is over-staffed and over-equipped, the cook and the governess counting as dairymaids, the estate-car and Land-Rover being classed as agricultural implements and their petrol consumption placed to the credit of some rarely operated tractor. In the second place, the farm's saleable production in poultry, eggs, milk, and fruit will prove a perpetual disappointment to all concerned. In so far as there is any profit from the company's total activities, it will be neatly swallowed up by directors' fees, which will admittedly be subject to tax but only as earned income and as distributed, moreover, among several closely related members of the Board.

The company which has been acquired rather than formed works on a different principle. In the taxation of companies, the tax collector looks to an average result over a number of years, allowing the profits of one year to be set against the losses of the years that are past. It follows that a company which has seen nothing but disaster and which is worthless to its proprietors, may be quite valuable to someone else. Its past losses can be advertised as an asset for sale, as something to offset future gains, and this is often done. The danger arises when the guaranteed loss turns out to include outstanding and undisclosed liabilities. Whether business enterprises are actually started for this purpose would be an interesting subject for inquiry. Tropically situated governments have sometimes offered a reward for the destruction of venomous snakes, usually on the basis of length, only to discover that the snakes were being bred for purposes of claiming the reward. In much the same way unsuccessful businesses, like antique furniture and vintage cars, may have to be manufactured. If we hear, therefore, of companies promoted for the sale of woollen underwear in equatorial Africa, or for the distribution of ice-cream in Lapland, we can fairly suspect that some such scheme has been launched.

If we turn now to consider the position of those without capital, we must remark that their plight is infinitely worse. To rise by legal means and enter the ranks of the socially privileged (except by marriage) is impracticable for all but a very few. To accumulate capital implies just such an excess of income over expenditure as the tax system seems designed to prevent. In many professions the young man makes little, the higher earnings being the reward for persistence in middle age. No allowance is made for this long apprenticeship, the income being fully taxed as soon as it becomes appreciable. When the moderately successful barrister has paid for his children's education and provided for his own old age he will be fortunate indeed to have much surplus. There is only one privileged profession in this respect, and that is the Civil Service. No other career offers such financial reward at so early an age, with honours and pension and nothing to lose.

When all the difficulties have been sufficiently emphasised, the fact remains that the feat of achieving financial independence is still occasionally performed by legal means.

For the purpose of investigating how this is done we must ignore, from the outset, the winners of sweepstakes and football pools. They may be and doubtless are an important new class in the classless society, but it would be unhelpful to urge the reader to join their ranks. To utter the advice 'Win the Irish Sweepstake' is no more useful than to say 'Be born the heir to the 16th Earl of Barsetshire and Blandings.' What is desirable is not always within reach. Our study must be confined rather to what is immediately feasible, and for this purpose we must return to first principles. Our concern is now solely with income, and we have seen already that income cannot escape taxation. So the problem is how legally to become more prosperous without receiving income, thus building up such a surplus as may be described, in the end, as capital. A little reflection will show that the desired result can be achieved in two ways, and most readily in fact by a combination of both. First, the income must be received, for the most part, in kind. Second, against the income in cash there must be set an equivalent and legally deductible loss.

In theory, and sometimes in practice, the most successful exponent of income avoidance is the subsistence farmer. What he makes is almost impossible to discover and what he loses will prove to be his almost sole topic of conversation. But what is possible for the true son of the soil is by no means as easy for anyone else. For the retired Brigadier or Group Captain, the likelihood is that his losses will be real and his income not theoretically but actually negative. The better policy is to engage not in agriculture but in business. The businessman can so arrange matters that his travel expenses, his entertainment of friends, his car and his flat, his wife and his daughter, are all provided for at the firm's expense. For tax purposes the only vehicle is a van, the flat an office, the wife a secretary, and the daughter a copy-typist, all travels are for promoting trade and all restaurant bills incurred while regaling clients. This largesse is as useful to the company as to the man it employs, for it all goes to reduce the tax payable on its profits.

With the tax avoider's income thus reduced to an insignificant figure, his next step is to extinguish that small total by an assumed burden of insurance premiums, annuities, mortgages, and trusts. With but average ingenuity an income can be made to vanish like the Cheshire Cat, leaving nothing behind but a self-satisfied grin, not strictly speaking liable to assessment. And a concealed income can gradually turn into capital. Remember, however, that the tax avoider must go soberly about his business, keeping his real expenses to the minimum. Observe too that his success in gaining prosperity will be due as much to his economy as to his skill in tax avoidance. To acquire capital, the basic method (apart from marrying money or gambling) is to limit expenditure while expanding income. To this policy a masterly avoidance of tax is essential but auxiliary. It is not itself the key to success.

One other word of warning must be uttered. The above-mentioned methods of tax avoidance are legal in theory but may well be challenged in practice. That the car is vital to the business may be more or less true, but the extent to which it is privately used could be a matter for argument. There might be dispute again about the secretary's travel expenses or the rent of the flat. Once your claim became the subject of litigation, the result would be a matter of chance. That being so, the safe rule is always to have as much money available as if the most pessimistic forecasts were sure to prove uniformly correct. For there can be nothing more fatal than to be in the tax collector's debt. By professing inability to pay at the time of demand, you make it virtually impossible to pay at all. When you produce the money, there is inevitably the question as to how you acquired it. If earned—and you can hardly claim that it was stolen—the sum paid is itself liable to tax. That new demand can be satisfied only by another payment, which is itself taxable; and so on indefinitely. It is by this chain of events that many a tax avoider is brought to ruin. We hear thus of one film actor who dare not set foot in the United States, of a novelist permanently exiled from Britain, of other people who slink around in dark spectacles and false beards, and of others again whose beards are genuine. Some distinguished people can escape from the toils only by bankruptcy or suicide. These clearly provide us with examples of a sort of policy we should do well to reject. The avoidance of tax demands, it is clear, a business acumen of the highest order.

While it is proper to emphasise that taxation can be avoided by the astute and worldly, we must also remember that many heirs to property are neither worldly nor astute. They include widows and orphans, Brigadiers and Wing Commanders, horse-lovers, dog-breeders, poets, and dons. People of this sort will often lack the business sense which alone could save them. Nor is this any matter for wonder. To survive in the jungle of tax-ridden finance, the classical scholar or horticulturalist would have to become a businessman, exchanging the lexicon or seed catalogue for the share list and prices current. Such a transformation is more feasible than might be supposed but brings with it a heavier penalty than many feel able to bear. The man who can save his rose garden only by devoting his energies to finance may fairly object that the rose garden, when saved, will no longer be his. In theory, the estate of an absent-minded philologist can be handled for him by a man of affairs. In practice, absence of mind will soon lead to absence of income. For businessmen it is relatively easy to buy from each other at a discount, enjoying an invisible income which is free of tax. But the scholar who attempts to do the same, and who succeeds, will no longer be a scholar. By saving his property he will have lost all reason for his existence. Many prefer to live their own chosen lives for as long as they can, sacrificing their financial independence rather than discarding, much sooner, their personal freedom.

Taxes that cannot be avoided can sometimes be evaded. While this chapter is in no sense a guide to tax evasion or even a commentary on the methods of tax evasion now in use, the reader can rest assured that taxes are evaded and that on a considerable scale. People who would describe themselves as law-abiding citizens, people who would un-hesitatingly assist the police during a riot, people who have served their country in war and peace, will readily falsify a tax return if they feel that this can be done with safety. They feel that the taxes are fixed on a penal scale by the votes of those whose own contribution will be small. They conclude that evasion is not only profitable but justified. It is this belief that transfers them by gradual stages from the ranks of the law-abiding to the ranks of the rebellious. Once a man has become accustomed to evading taxation, once he has come to regard the policeman as a possible danger and not as an ally, he will begin to show less respect for any kind of law. In the days of prohibition the smuggler of liquor ended as a murderer. From breaking a law which everyone could see to be senseless he went on to break every other law there was. On a smaller scale, the tax laws are having something like the same effect.

That some otherwise law-abiding people would evade taxes in any case is undoubtedly true, but their number would be small if their margin of profit were less. With a tax of about 10 per cent of income, the cost of evasion (or even of avoidance) becomes for most people more than the amount of the tax. Even with tax at 20 per cent, the skill now devoted to evading the tax might be more profitably directed towards increasing the income. And, given anything like an even choice, the average citizen would rather give his money to the State than to a group of lawyers, accountants, advisers and experts. It is less trouble, for one thing, and he may feel generally sympathetic towards many of the objects in view. It is the widening of the gap between the cost of evasion and the far higher cost of the tax that tends, eventually, to make criminals out of honest men. In many parts of Britain people overestimate the strength of the law. They feel that the forces of civilisation are absolutely in the ascendant and have little to fear from subversion or crime. Those who have lived in, say, Liverpool, have no such illusions. They realise that civilisation is precarious and widely in abeyance after sunset. They know, as others cannot, that, with the battle so evenly matched, we cannot afford to drive even wavering adherents into the enemy's camp.

While the whole question of tax avoidance and evasion must hinge on the ratio between the cost of avoidance (or evasion) and the amount of the tax, there is one other factor of which little notice has been taken. The taxpayer's reluctance to pay has been strengthened in recent years by his growing conviction that the money he pays will be largely wasted. This was not true to the same extent in former ages. The earliest rulers of civilised states might be guilty, at times, of personal extravagance, but this is not to be confused with waste in the modern sense. It could not be said of palaces, pleasure grounds, costly robes, dancing girls, concubines, elaborate food and rare wine, that they were exactly wasted. They might be consumed, they might be discarded; but what else, after all, is anyone to do with them? Insufficient use of the facilities available would certainly have been wasteful. But it is not, in the main, a story of such neglect that history has to tell; nor, incidentally, would the taxpayer of the ancient world have been particularly pleased by a display of economy at court. He could share in fabulous pleasures to the extent of hearing them described, and for any but the most meanly envious there is a satisfaction in vicarious luxury which is not to be derived from a tale of thrift. Kings could economise, to be sure, over the dancing girls' attire, and often seem to have done so; but parsimonious rulers were never loved and even those merely luxurious were felt to be serving a purpose of some kind.

In modern times there has been relatively little extravagance of this picturesque sort; so little, indeed, that Adam Smith, for one, scarcely mentions its possible effect. In laying down principles of taxation, he emphasised equality of incidence, certainty in method, convenience of form, and economy in collection. He saw less reason to insist that the sums collected should not be too obviously thrown away. But that nowadays is becoming a principal point at issue. In place of the expenses which used to arise from what a few would regard as extravagance we now have far heavier expenses arising from what everyone can see to be futile. The wastefulness of government is thus becoming a major factor in the situation. It is one thing to pay taxes for objects which all must agree to be necessary. It is quite another to pay for what is needless, harmful, or absurd.

CAREERS

7

Short List
or Principles of Selection

A PROBLEM CONSTANTLY BEFORE THE MODERN ADMIN-
istration, whether in government or business, is that of
personnel selection. The inexorable working of Parkinson's
Law ensures that appointments have constantly to be made
and the question is always how to choose the right candidate from all who present themselves. In ascertaining the
principles upon which the choice should be made, we may
properly consider, under separate heads, the methods used
in the past and the methods used at the present day.

Past methods, not entirely disused, fall into two main
categories, the British and the Chinese. Both deserve careful consideration, if only for the reason that they were
obviously more successful than any method now considered fashionable. The British method (old pattern) depended
upon an interview in which the candidate had to establish
his identity. He would be confronted by elderly gentlemen
seated round a mahogany table who would presently ask

him his name. Let us suppose that the candidate replied, 'John Seymour.' One of the gentlemen would then say, 'Any relation to the Duke of Somerset?' To this the candidate would say, quite possibly, 'No, sir.' Then another gentleman would say, 'Perhaps you are related, in that case, to the Bishop of Watminster?' If he said 'No, sir' again, a third would ask in despair, 'To whom then *are* you related?' In the event of the candidate's saying, 'Well, my father is a fishmonger in Cheapside,' the interview was virtually over. The members of the Board would exchange significant glances, one would press a bell and another tell the footman, 'Throw this person out.' One name could be crossed off the list without further discussion. Supposing the next candidate was Henry Molyneux and a nephew of the Earl of Sefton, his chances remained fair up to the moment when George Howard arrived and proved to be a grandson of the Duke of Norfolk. The Board encountered no serious difficulty until they had to compare the claims of the third son of a baronet with the second but illegitimate son of a viscount. Even then they could refer to a Book of Precedence. So their choice was made and often with the best results.

The Admiralty version of this British method (old pattern) was different only in its more restricted scope. The Board of Admirals were unimpressed by titled relatives as such. What they sought to establish was a service connection. The ideal candidate would reply to the second question, 'Yes, Admiral Parker is my uncle. My father is Captain Foley, my grandfather Commodore Foley. My mother's father was Admiral Hardy. Commander Hardy is my uncle. My eldest brother is a Lieutenant in the Royal Marines, my next brother is a cadet at Dartmouth and my younger brother wears a sailor suit.' 'Ah!' the senior Admiral would say. 'And what made you think of joining the Navy?' The answer to this question, however, would scarcely matter, the clerk present having already noted the candidate as acceptable. Given a choice between two candidates, both equally acceptable by birth, a member of the Board would ask suddenly, 'What was the number of the taxi you came in?' The candidate who said 'I came by bus' was then thrown out. The candidate who said, truthfully, 'I don't know' was rejected, and the candidate who said 'Number 2351' (lying) was promptly admitted to the service as a boy with initiative. This method often produced excellent results.

The British method (new pattern) was evolved in the late 19th century as something more suitable for a democratic country. The Selection Committee would ask briskly, 'What school were you at?' and would be told Harrow, Haileybury, or Rugby, as the case might be. 'What games do you play?' would be the next and invariable question. A promising candidate would reply, 'I have played tennis for England, cricket for Yorkshire, rugby for the Harlequins, and fives for Winchester.' The next question would then be 'Do you play polo?'—just to prevent the candidate's thinking too highly of himself. Even without playing polo, however, he was evidently worth serious consideration. Little time, by contrast, was wasted on the man who admitted to having been educated at Wiggleworth. 'Where?' the chairman would ask in astonishment, and 'Where's that?' after the name had been repeated. 'Oh, in *Lancashire*!' he would say at last. Just for a matter of form, some member might ask, 'What games do you play?' But the reply 'Table tennis for Wigan, cycling for Blackpool, and snooker for Wiggleworth' would finally have his name deleted from the list. There might even be some muttered comment upon people who deliberately wasted the com-

mittee's time. Here again was a method which produced good results.

The Chinese method (old pattern) was at one time so exentisvely copied by other nations that few people realise its Chinese origin. This is the method of Competitive Written Examination. In China under the Ming Dynasty the more promising students used to sit for the provincial examination, held every third year. It lasted three sessions of three days each. During the first session the candidate wrote three essays and composed a poem of eight couplets. During the second session he wrote five essays on a classical theme. During the third, he wrote five essays on the art of government. The successful candidates (perhaps two per cent) then sat for their final examination at the imperial capital. It lasted only one session, the candidates writing one essay on a current political problem. Of those who were successful the majority were admitted to the civil service, the man with the highest marks being destined for the highest office. The system worked fairly well.

The Chinese system was studied by Europeans between 1815 and 1830 and adopted by the East India Company in 1832. The effectiveness of this method was investigated by a committee in 1854, with Macaulay as chairman. The result was that the system of competitive examination was introduced into the Civil Service in 1855. An essential feature of the Chinese examinations had been their literary character. The test was in a knowledge of the classics, in an ability to write elegantly (both prose and verse), and in the stamina necessary to complete the course. All these features were faithfully incorporated in the Trevelyan-Northcote Report, and thereafter in the system it did so much to create. It was assumed that classical learning and literary ability would fit any candidate for any administrative post. It was assumed (no doubt rightly) that a scientific education would fit a candidate for nothing—except, possibly, science. It was known, finally, that it is virtually impossible to find an order of merit among people who have been examined in different subjects. Since it is impracticable to decide whether one man is better in geology than another man in physics, it is at least convenient to be able to rule them both out as useless. When all candidates alike have to write Greek or Latin verse, it is relatively easy to decide which verse is the best. Men thus selected on their classical performance were then sent forth to govern India. Those with lower marks were retained to govern England. Those with still lower marks were rejected altogether or sent to the colonies. While it would be totally wrong to describe this system as a failure, no one could claim for it the success that had attended the systems hitherto in use. There was no guarantee, to begin with, that the man with the highest marks might not turn out to be off his head; as was sometimes found to be the case. Then again the writing of Greek verse might prove to be the sole accomplishment that some candidates had or would ever have. On occasion, a successful applicant may even have been impersonated at the examination by someone else, subsequently proving unable to write Greek verse when the occasion arose. Selection by a competitive examination was never therefore more than a moderate success.

Whatever the faults, however, of the competitive written examination, it certainly produced better results than any method that has been attempted since. Modern methods centre upon the intelligence test and the psychological interview. The defect in the intelligence test is that high marks are gained by those who subsequently prove to be practically illiterate. So much time has been spent in studying the art of being tested that the candidate has rarely had time for anything else. The psychological interview has developed today into what is known as ordeal by house party. The candidates spend a pleasant weekend under expert observation. As one of them trips over the doormat and says 'Bother!' examiners lurking in the background whip out their notebooks and jot down, 'Poor physical co-ordination' and 'Lacks self-control.' There is no need to describe this method in detail, but its results are all about us and are obviously deplorable. The persons who satisfy this type of examiner are usually of a cautious and suspicious temperament, pedantic and smug, saying little and doing nothing. It is quite common, when appointments are made by this method, for one man to be chosen from five hundred applicants, only to be sacked a few weeks later as useless even beyond the standards of his department. Of the various methods of selection so far tried, the latest is unquestionably the worst.

What method should be used in the future? A clue to a

possible line of investigation is to be found in one little-publicised aspect of contemporary selective technique. So rarely has the occasion arisen for appointing a Chinese translator to the Foreign Office that the method used is little known. The post is advertised and the applications go, let us suppose, to a committee of five. Three are civil servants and two are Chinese scholars of great eminence. Heaped on the table before this committee are 483 forms of application, with testimonials attached. All the applicants are Chinese and all without exception have a first degree from Peking or Amoy and a Doctorate of Philosophy from Cornell or Johns Hopkins. The majority of the candidates have at one time held ministerial office in Taiwan. Some have attached their photographs. Others have (perhaps wisely) refrained from doing so. The chairman turns to the leading Chinese expert and says, 'Perhaps Dr Wu can tell us which of these candidates should be put on the short list.' Dr Wu smiles enigmatically and points to the heap. 'None of them any good,' he says briefly. 'But how—I mean, why not?' asks the chairman, surprised. 'Because no good scholar would ever apply. He would fear to lose face if he were not chosen.' 'So what do we do now?' asks the chairman. 'I think,' says Dr Wu, 'we might persuade Dr Lim to take this post. What do you think, Dr Lee?' 'Yes, I think he might,' says Lee, 'but we couldn't approach him ourselves of course. We could ask Dr Tan whether he thinks Dr Lim would be interested.' 'I don't know Dr Tan,' says Wu, 'but I know his friend Dr Wong.' By then the chairman is too muddled to know who is to be approached by whom. But the great thing is that *all* the applications are thrown into the waste-paper basket, only one candidate being considered, and he a man who did not apply.

We do not advise the universal adoption of the modern

Chinese method but we draw from it the useful conclusion that the failure of other methods is mainly due to there being too many candidates. There are, admittedly, some initial steps by which the total may be reduced. The formula 'Reject everyone over 50 or under 20 plus everyone who is Irish' is now universally used, and its application will somewhat reduce the list. The names remaining will still, however, be too numerous. To choose between three hundred people, all well qualified and highly recommended, is not really possible. We are driven therefore to conclude that the mistake lies in the original advertisement. It has attracted too many applications. The disadvantage of this is so little realised that people devise advertisements in terms which will inevitably attract thousands. A post of responsibility is announced as vacant, the previous occupant being now in the House of Lords. The salary is large, the pension generous, the duties nominal, the privileges immense, the perquisites valuable, free residence provided with official car, and unlimited facilities for travel. Candidates should apply, promptly but carefully, enclosing copies (not originals) of not more than three recent testimonials. What is the result? A deluge of applications, many from lunatics and as many again from retired army majors with a gift (as they always claim) for handling men. There is nothing to do except burn the lot and start thinking all over again. It would have saved time and trouble to do some thinking in the first place.

Only a little thought is needed to convince us that the perfect advertisement would attract only one reply and that from the right man. Let us begin with an extreme example:

Wanted: Acrobat capable of crossing a slack wire 200 feet above raging furnace. Twice nightly, three times on Saturday.

Salary offered £250 per week. No pension and no compensation in the event of injury. Apply in person at Wildcat Circus between the hours of 9 a.m. and 10 a.m.

The wording of this may not be perfect but the *aim* should be so to balance the inducement in salary against the possible risks involved that only a single applicant will appear. It is needless to ask for details for qualifications and experience. No one unskilled on the slack wire would find the offer attractive. It is needless to insist that candidates should be physically fit, sober, and free from fits of dizziness. They know that. It is just as needless to stipulate that those nervous of heights need not apply. They won't. The skill of the advertiser consists in adjusting the salary to the danger. An offer of £1,000 per week might produce a dozen applicants. An offer of £15 might produce none. Somewhere between those two figures lies the exact sum to specify, the minimum figure to attract anyone actually capable of doing the job. If there is more than one applicant, the figure has been placed a trifle too high.

Let us now take, for comparison, a less extreme example:

Wanted: An archaeologist with high academic qualifications willing to spend fifteen years in excavating the Inca tombs at Helsdump on the Alligator River. Knighthood or equivalent honour guaranteed. Pension payable but never yet claimed. Salary of £6,000 per year. Apply in triplicate to the Director of the Grubbenburrow Institute, Sickdale, Ill., U.S.A.

Here the advantages and drawbacks are neatly balanced. There is no need to insist that candidates must be patient, tough, intrepid, and single. The terms of the advertisement have eliminated all who are not. It is unnecessary to require that candidates must be mad on excavating tombs.

Mad is just what they will certainly be. Having thus reduced the possible applicants to a maximum of about three, the terms of the advertisement place the salary just too low to attract two of them and the promised honour *just* high enough to interest the third. We may suppose that, in this case, the offer of a K.C.M.G. would have produced two applications, the offer of an O.B.E. none. The result is a single candidate. He is off his head but that does not matter. He is the man we want.

It may be thought that the world offers comparatively few opportunities to appoint slack-wire acrobats and tomb excavators, and that the problem is more often to find candidates for less exotic appointments. This is true, but the same principles can be applied. Their application demands, however—as is evident—a greater degree of skill. Let us suppose that the post to be filled is that of Prime Minister. The modern tendency is to trust in various methods of election, with results that are almost invariably disastrous. Were we to turn, instead, to the fairy stories we learned in childhood, we should realise that at the period to which these stories relate far more satisfactory methods were in use. When the king had to choose a man to marry his eldest or only daughter and so inherit the kingdom, he normally planned some obstacle course from which only the right candidate would emerge with credit; and from which indeed (in many instances) only the right candidate emerged at all. For imposing such a test the kings of that rather vaguely defined period were well provided with both personnel and equipment. Their establishment included magicians, demons, fairies, vampires, werewolves, giants, and dwarfs. Their territories were supplied with magic mountains, rivers of fire, hidden treasures, and enchanted forests. It might be urged that modern governments are in this respect less fortunate. This, however, is by no means certain. An administrator able to command the services of psychologists, psychiatrists, alienists, statisticians, and efficiency experts is not perhaps in a worse (or better) position than one relying upon hideous crones and fairy godmothers. An administration equipped with movie cameras, television apparatus, radio networks, and X-ray machines would not appear to be in a worse (or better) position than one employing magic wands, crystal balls, wishing wells, and cloaks of invisibility. Their means of assessment would seem, at any rate, to be strictly comparable. All that is required is to translate the technique of the fairy story into a form applicable to the modern world. In this, as we shall see, there is no essential difficulty.

The first step in the process is to decide on the qualities a Prime Minister ought to have. These need not be the same in all circumstances, but they need to be listed and agreed upon. Let us suppose that the qualities deemed essential are (1) Energy, (2) Courage, (3) Patriotism, (4) Experience, (5) Popularity, and (6) Eloquence. Now, it will be observed that all these are general qualities which all possible applicants would believe themselves to possess. The field could readily, of course, be narrowed by stipulating (4) Experience *of lion-taming*, or (6) Eloquence *in Mandarin*. But that is not the way in which we want to narrow the field. We do not want to stipulate a quality in a special form; rather, each quality in an exceptional degree. In other words, the successful candidate must be the most energetic, courageous, patriotic, experienced, popular, and eloquent man in the country. Only one man can answer to that description and his is the only application we want. The terms of the appointment must thus be phrased so as to exclude everyone else. We should therefore word the advertisement in some such way as follows:

Wanted: Prime Minister of Ruritania. Hours of work: 4 a.m. to 11:59 p.m. Candidates must be prepared to fight three rounds with the current heavyweight champion (regulation gloves to be worn). Candidates will die for their country, by painless means, on reaching the age of retirement (65). They will have to pass an examination in parliamentary procedure and will be liquidated should they fail to obtain 95 per cent marks. They will also be liquidated if they fail to gain 75 per cent votes in a popularity poll held under the Gallup Rules. They will finally be invited to try their eloquence on a Baptist Congress, the object being to induce those present to rock and roll. Those who fail will be liquidated. All candidates should present themselves at the Sporting Club (side entrance) at 11:15 a.m. on the morning of September 19. Gloves will be provided, but they should bring their own rubber-soled shoes, singlet, and shorts.

Observe that this advertisement saves all trouble about application forms, testimonials, photographs, references, and short lists. If the advertisement has been correctly worded, there will be only one applicant, and he can take office immediately—well, almost immediately. But what if there is no applicant? That is proof that the advertisement needs rewording. We have evidently asked for something more than exists. So the same advertisement (which is, after all, quite economical in space) can be inserted again with some slight adjustment. The pass mark in the examination can be reduced to 85 per cent with 65 per cent of the votes required in the popularity poll, and only two rounds against the heavyweight champion. Conditions can be successively relaxed, indeed, until an applicant appears.

Suppose, however, that two or even three candidates present themselves. We shall know that we have been insufficiently scientific. It may be that the pass mark in the examination has been too abruptly lowered—it should have been 87 per cent, perhaps, with 66 per cent in the popularity poll. Whatever the cause, the damage has been done. Two, or possibly three, candidates are in the waiting room. We have a choice to make and cannot waste all the morning on it. One policy would be to start the ordeal and eliminate the candidates who emerge with least credit. There is, nevertheless, a quicker way. Let us assume that all three candidates have all the qualities already defined as essential. The only thing we need do is add one further quality and apply the simplest test of all. To do this, we ask the nearest young lady (receptionist or typist, as the case may be), 'Which would you prefer?' She will promptly point out one of the candidates and so finish the matter. It has been objected that this procedure is the same thing as tossing a coin or otherwise letting chance decide. There is, in fact, no element of chance. It is merely the last-minute insistence on one other quality, one not so far taken into account: the quality of sex appeal.

8

Secundity
or Below the Summit

A TIME MAY COME FOR ANY MAN WHEN HE FINDS THE
summit within reach. Suppose you stand second in the
hierarchy and may soon (who knows?) be first. You will
have played second fiddle before but not at this rarefied
altitude. The time has come for that last great effort on
which your future must depend. How to be the perfect
Number Two? Here is a question demanding the most
careful analysis. We are faced at the outset, however, with
a problem of nomenclature. By what official title is your
secundity to be defined? Terms of status are apt to prove
misleading and fluid. Behind their imprecisions there loom,
however, the hard facts of life. In nearly every big
organisation there is a Number One. There is also, and
almost as inevitably, a Number Two.

There they are and have always been, and there presum-
ably they will always be. In primitive societies the family
group is headed by the father or the grandfather, 'the old

man' (as a ship's Master is still called) to whom his eldest son stands as Number Two, deputy, and presumed successor. All human authority has this paternal origin, being based on wonder, affection, and fear; wonder felt by a child when witnessing his father's skill, affection for a protector who is interested in securing the child's survival, and fear of the punishment in which the father, as teacher, is bound to inflict. The office of Number Two, or eldest (or, alternatively, ablest) son has thus a respectable antiquity.

But does *every* organisation have an acknowledged Number Two? No, there is a significant exception. In a political despotism or dictatorship there is no real deputy and no named successor. For the whole strength of the regime rests on the assumption that the current ruler is impossible to replace. After all, an effective deputy makes the ruler less indispensable. A known successor makes him less secure. It is part of the technique, therefore, of dictatorship to leave the second throne unfilled. Instead of Number Two there are several people in competition, the position of each weakened by the jealousy of the rest. Nor is dictatorship unknown in commerce and industry. There have been Corporations ruled in much the same way and usually with the same result; namely, that the organisation lasts no longer than the man. The normal preference of mankind is for institutions of greater stability, for types of government which can survive a single bullet, for industrial empires which can survive a single heart attack. So that industrial dictatorships are more the exception than the rule.

Another exception to the norm is to be found where the Number Two is really the Number One. The whisper goes round that Mr Lurking is the man to see if you want results—not Mr Roger de Coverley, Managing Director though he may be. This sort of situation is not uncommon.

There are men like Mr Lurking who hunger for power but not for office and they sometimes contrive to join forces with someone like Coverley, who longs for office but not for power. It was thus at one time the German Army custom to select a Chief-of-Staff with meticulous care, appointing his Commander-in-Chief as a careless afterthought. There are examples, moreover, of such an inverted partnership proving successful, as it might often prove in a society merely of men. Among a celibate priesthood, as with a Cardinal and his confessor, this arrangement may often work well. But where one man is married there is an element of instability in the relationship; and where both are married there are two. The married chief who is dominated by his Number Two is also likely to be dominated by his wife; and she, resenting a rival's influence, will urge her husband to assert himself. Number Two's wife may be more submissive to Number Two but her grievance will lie in the almost insufferable airs of superiority assumed by the wife of Number One. The influence of the Bishop's lady in Trollope's novel was greater than that of the Bishop's chaplain, not merely because she was more formidable but because she was more constantly at the Bishop's side. So it is in real life. And even were both men bachelors, who can guarantee that they will so remain? Where a single red-haired and pert-nosed secretary can bring about an internal revolution, the situation lacks stability. The pyramid stands better with its apex at the top.

Taking, then, the normal and preferable situation where Number One is actually as well as theoretically in charge, we must now consider the position of Number Two. Our temptation at the outset is to conclude that all Numbers Two are alike. It is so easy to picture the ideal Number Two—old Tom, old Dick, or old Harry, so *reliable,* so quietly efficient, always there when wanted, so tactfully absent when not required, so kind to the office staff, and such a delightful uncle to Number One's children. But such incidental functions as these must not be allowed to cloud our vision. Numbers Two are *not* all the same. Some are self-effacing and obscure, others are mysterious and secretive. There is the Number Two who is genial but evasive and the opposite type who is negative and dumb. Some are effusively co-operative but foiled, it would seem, by the opposition of the Board. Others are obstructive and surly until outflanked by an appeal to higher authority. Numbers Two might seem, in fact, to offer an infinite variety in temperament and outlook. They actually fall, however, into two basic categories: those (A) who are content to be Number Two and those (B) who want to become Number One. It might not be easy to draw a firm line between the one category and the other—for some individuals are to be found in a state of transition—but the

categories exist and the majority of Numbers Two can be placed in one or the other.

The inevitable and eternal Numbers Two, who lack, and perhaps have always lacked, any higher ambition, are easily distinguishable. They reveal a slight wandering of interest, a preoccupation with things not strictly within the organisation. They talk of Ratepayers' Associations, Boards, local politics, Golf Clubs, and the Chamber of Commerce. Their homes reveal an assumption that they will always be there—as in the cultivation of asparagus and the concreting of the drive. They are as active as ever, mind you—never more so—and never (well, hardly ever) late at the office. But they have passed the age of ambition and have begun to take a pride, rather, in the progress of their children; in their son's success at Oxford or their married daughter's firstborn. There is a settled, comfortable look about the predestined Number Two. He is to be identified more by that than by anything he says. From force of habit he may even go on talking of promotion but his words are belied by his appearance.

There is an art in being the contented Number Two, whether as one predestined from the start or as one whose role has been thrust upon him. It is the art, essentially, of identifying oneself with a hero. At the cinema or before the television screen the normal person will readily identify himself with the hero of the moment. He does not visualize the Western set at the studio and the director ordering a tenth retake of the first sequence. He does not wonder why people should always fall when hit and nevertheless rise unhurt. He just clenches his fists or allows his hand to hover over an imaginary holster, seeing the hero's prowess as his own. The ideal Number Two makes Number One his hero and assumes for himself a share of the drama. It is 'we' who take the decision and 'we' who quell the absurd proposals put forward at the Board Meeting. 'Number One knows all that goes on,' says Number Two. 'You can't fool *him*. He knows all the answers.' But the tone of his admiration cannot hide from us the fact that Number Two has projected himself into the part. Number One's achievement has become partly his. And Numbers Two (A) although they may differ at the outset, tend to become alike as time goes on. It is thus the duty of a Chief-of-Staff to write in the style of his Commander-in-Chief, so choosing his words that the despatch hardly needs alteration. The ideal Number Two speaks with the voice of his chief and has no separate views of his own.

Come now to category B, the probably larger group of Numbers Two whose ambition is to be Number One. These executives can be divided into three groups, (I), (II), and (III). Those in Group I were all appointed *since* Number One. Chosen by Number One himself from among the departmental heads, this type of deputy seems relatively young and optimistic, never (he says) having expected such promotion and never having held such high office before. 'Gosh!' he will explain. 'But it's splendid to work under a man like Alan Topleigh! I learn something new every day. He's a wonderful chap—and he does know his stuff! I know when I'm lucky.' Bubbling over with devotion, especially when within earshot of Mrs Topleigh, Bob Upton is obviously a Coming Man. He can't think why the chief should have picked on *him*, with so many good men to choose from, but there it is. Alan shall never regret his choice, not if Bob can help it. When Alan is away at a Conference, Bob shines as deputy. 'No,' he says, 'I don't think that is the decision that Alan would have made.' 'Yes,' he admits, 'that's pretty much in line with our policy.' 'As for that last item,' he concludes, 'I feel that had better wait until Alan gets back.' And when

Alan Topleigh talks about retirement, it is Bob who leads the deputation that implores him to stay on. 'Maybe you need a holiday, sir, but we all want you back here at your desk. We still need you and we can't believe you're ready to retire.' Everyone agrees that Bob Upton is a first-rate fellow and that his star is in the ascendant.

In Group II are the Numbers Two who were appointed *before* Number One assumed his present post. Each was the choice of Number One's predecessor. Mark Waydown is a good example of a Number Two (B.II). He is the very best type of executive, efficient, co-operative, and popular. Rumour has it that the Board took a chance on the present Number One, Mr Picton Young, and would never have done so had they not been able to rely on Waydown—the ideal man to help a chief whose experience (at that time) was hardly sufficient. And no one can deny that Mark ('Daddy' to the juniors) has done a splendid job. He is not really so much older than Number One but he often seems elderly by comparison—and just a little inclined to fuss. But the organisation would be nowhere, simply *nowhere* without him. If anyone knows the business, it is he. He knows everyone by name and is always ready with advice or help. It is he who remembers that a scheme like the one under discussion was tried before in 1937. If there is a complex job to do, Mark is the man to tackle it. He takes a simple pride in the way he is trusted by the Board. No one has ever questioned his loyalty to Number One, even though some believe him to be the abler man of the two. 'Leave it to Mark,' says Number One, and the job, whatever it is, will be finished in time. If the firm's output can be said to depend on any one individual, Mark would be that man; or so most people think. He is more than valuable, he is *essential*.

In the same category and group as Mark Waydown but

in a different industry is Carveth Carping, unquestionably one of the ablest executives in the Bellectronics business. Of Carping's ability there can be no doubt at all. He would have been Managing Director if Victor Peake had not happened to be available. A little older than Mark Waydown and looking older than he is, Carveth has never been more than civil to Victor. Eight years his junior, the Managing Director makes a show of friendly informality but it deceives nobody. As for Carveth, he overflows with unspoken criticism. Asked about the Company's policy, he outlines the current plan for development, shrugs his shoulders and adds, after a slight pause, 'Whether this scheme is the best we can do . . . well, time will show. Some of us have sometimes—oh, well, it doesn't matter now. You know Peake, of course? A remarkable man! I don't know how he does it—I really don't!' He is often heard to say, 'I don't know how he does it!' and there is just enough ambiguity about this to create despondency. Without uttering a word which could be called disloyal, Carveth throws doubts on each decision the chief takes. 'If we didn't *trust* Peake as we do, we might *almost* think he had misjudged the market trend, but I suppose he must know what he's doing. He has a sort of intuition, and that's more valuable, I dare say, than mere experience. We shall see . . .' Carveth is a master of pregnant silence—he could have taken his degree in it—and his raised eyebrows convey more distrust than words could express. From all Carveth omits to say, it is obvious that Peake's failure is complete.

Last of all, there is Group III, comprising former Numbers One, brought into the organisation as the result of a merger. There is Brian Boughtover, for example, who became Number Two of the Giantsquid Group when his own Company (Frankleigh, Tottering & Co.) was absorbed in 1960. Relations between the Managing Director and

Brian are too polite to be convincing. 'Let's ask Brian's opinion before we go any further,' says Cecil Summit. 'Oh, no, Cecil,' says Brian, 'your judgment is best—I would rather be guided by you.' 'Thank you, Brian, but you have more experience in this particular field.' 'I wouldn't say that, Cecil—I believe you know more than any of us.' 'You are too modest, Brian,' etc., etc. So the discussion goes on, Cecil devoutly wishing that Brian were not there, and Brian wishing as fervently that he were somewhere else. The Number One reduced in rank presents a frequent problem in the world of business and one to which there is usually only one solution: Brian's retirement or transfer.

If we analyse and compare the present position of these four representative Numbers Two, we realise at once that Bob Upton is the only one certain of promotion. In the ordinary way, we should expect him to leave shortly in order to accept the Managing Directorship of a smaller concern in the same line of business. This appointment will be on Alan Topleigh's recommendation, his private letter emphasising that Bob is the best man he has ever trained. Three years later, Topleigh will retire and Bob will be his obvious successor. No such good fortune awaits Mark Waydown, who is indispensable (as Number Two). Picton Young will never release him. Should Mark put in for the top post elsewhere, at his wife's insistence, Picton's letter of recommendation will lay stress on his loyalty and competence while subtly throwing doubt on his fitness to be Number One. 'As actual head of an organisation, Mr Waydown is untried, but of this I am certain, that he will always do his utmost.' With this kind of support, Mark is sure of second place on any short list, and second he will remain unless the man chosen should actually burst a blood vessel and drop dead on being offered the post. The question often asked is whether Mark really wants more

responsibility than he has. Who can tell? Certainly not
Mark himself, in whom disappointment and relief are nicely
balanced. The truth is, maybe, that he was more ambitious
to begin with and is less ambitious now. But rejecting an
applicant is very much a matter of habit. Whoever has
been rejected once will usually be rejected again. And
whoever has been passed over once, the appointment going
to a younger man, will *certainly* be passed over again. To
appoint him on a later occasion would be tantamount to
admitting that the earlier rejection was a mistake; which is
absurd. So Mark's chances of promotion are in inverse
proportion to his present usefulness. His chances are dwindling and will presently vanish.

But Mark's chances, slight as they are, look hopeful
when compared with those of Carveth Carping. The position of these two men is basically the same (B.II), each
having seen a younger man preferred. It is their reaction
that has been different. To the man passed over, two
obvious courses are open. He can show by his loyal co-
operation that there is no vice in him. Or else he can show,
by proof of superior intelligence, that the decision against
him was unquestionably wrong. Either course is fatal but
the latter more immediately so. For the mutual dislike
between Peake and Carping must produce a state of dead-
lock. Carping would go, as Number One, to a smaller
company, but Peake will never support his claim. In theory, Peake should be anxious to get rid of him and so
indeed he is. But this anxiety is seldom so strongly felt as
to produce a glowing testimonial. Carping's actual promotion is too high a price to pay for his removal. The mutual
loathing felt for each other by Peake and Carping is the
force, in fact, which keeps them together. And were Peake
to find the situation intolerable he would almost certainly
frustrate himself in a different way. For his letters of

support would become too effusive as well as too numerous.
Beyond a certain point enthusiasm arouses suspicion.

'If this chap is really such a ball of fire why is Peake so
keen to get rid of him?'

'Maybe he makes Peake feel small.'

'In that case we can't give much weight to Peake's
recommendation. Let's have another look at Ratrace again,
the Number Two at Savage, Striving, Ltd.' So Carping is
not even placed. And the more consistently he is proved
right, the further down the list does his name appear. Who
wants a man who is always saying 'I told you so'? In the
ordinary course of events Carping is doomed to frustration.
Had he been made Number One in the first place he would
have been as good as Peake or better. But disappointment
has spoilt his character as well as his prospects. He is no
longer in the hunt.

And what of Brian Boughtover? His prospects are relatively good. There is a certain fraternity among Numbers
One, a feeling of club membership. Once in, you are
always in, at least for some purposes; and once out, you
stand a fair chance of re-admission. If Brian is not too near
the age of retirement he will have Summit's help towards a
new position as Number One. It will not do to have former
Numbers One on the labour market. It lowers the status of
the others, serving as a reminder of what can befall any
one of them. There is an unspoken rule that the man
displaced should, if possible, be hauled back on to the raft.
What is least desirable is to have Brian still there as
Number Two.

From this study of Numbers Two (A) who are content as
they are, and Numbers Two (B) who long for promotion,
it will be apparent that the role to avoid is that of a
Number Two (B) to whom promotion is denied. So much
is clear enough: but what if this is the role that has been

thrust upon you? It can happen to any of us. So let the reader suppose, for a minute, that it has happened to him. You have been rejected for the top post, let us imagine, and the man chosen is six years your junior. You might yourself be content, in time, to remain Number Two, but your wife is NOT content to be the Number Two Wife. She has begun to give you the pitying glance which is reserved for the world's predestined Numbers Two. Your daughter has been heard to refer to you as 'Poor old pop.' The situation is serious, not to say critical, and it is a case of Now or Never. What are you to do?

The starting-point for your pondering is this question: *'Were they right to pass you over?'* So far, in discussing the position of Mark Waydown, Carveth Carping, Bob Upton, and Brian Boughtover, we have assumed that all these Numbers Two are capable, or were once capable, of being Number One. There are many Numbers Two of whom this can fairly be said. But there are others, equally ambitious and undoubtedly able, who would fail if promoted. Nor shall we understand the essential character of a Number Two unless we can analyse his shortcoming. What distinguishes the natural Number One from the inevitable but frustrated Number Two? You are too modest to press your own claims so we shall ask your wife whether the Board was right to reject you. Suppose that her reply is on these lines:

'Right? Are you crazy? Everyone knows that Tony is the better man. He has been the brains of the business for years. After all, he ought to understand the trade, having joined the staff in 1946, just when he came out of the Navy. How he worked in those early days, when we were first married! He used to work all night so as to have the answer ready when the boss wanted some information. Tony is a worker all right. And then, everyone likes him.

Yes, *everyone*. There is never a grumble if Tony says that people must stay on at the office. They know that it must be necessary, and they know that he'll be the last to leave. Though I say it myself, Tony is the very best man they could have chosen. And what do they do? They find this Upward fellow and his cheap-looking wife. It's the craziest thing they ever did.'

Let us suppose that all she says is true. You are all she thinks and more. But we still have no proof that you are Number One material. *Are you?* It is your own answer to this question that is important. You must believe in yourself before others can believe in you. Your own verdict comes first and it may be final. Newspapers sometimes carry self-marking questionnaires in which people are invited to assess their own qualities, often on the basis of twenty questions or more. For you, for the man who has already come so far towards success, for a perfectly competent Number Two, there are only three questions, and they are as follows:

QUESTION ONE: *When you have a cold or high temperature, on what day of the week does it begin?* Think back carefully. Maybe you will answer, 'Well it might begin any day, I suppose. Can't say I've really noticed.' If that is your answer, Number Two is your right level. For the predestined Number One will answer without hesitation: 'All my ailments begin on Friday afternoon and I always recover by Monday morning.' The point is that a Number Two destined to be Number One must never go sick, or not at least until years after his promotion. Everyone else can have influenza if they like and can have it during the same week, as they often do, but that makes it all the more vital that *you* should be there. And at your desk you will be found, let the epidemic be what it may.

But can the onset of an illness be thus controlled by the patient? It certainly can. You make no deliberate effort but in the natural boss (if you are one) the ailment is subconsciously held in check. There is some internal mechanism which keeps the germs on the leash from Monday to Friday. 'You can't be ill now,' it whispers, 'there's the staff meeting this afternoon.' 'There's the lunch for Lord Dimwit,' it hisses. 'You can't begin sneezing yet.' This built-in mechanism works perfectly until Friday midday. Although no longer on top form, you deal with all the urgent business and begin signing the outgoing mail at about 3:30. It is then that your secretary observes for the first time that you are not looking well. As she comments on this, using that tone of motherly solicitude which she was made to rehearse at the Secretarial College, you sneeze. 'Oh, dear, Mr Toplevel, I do believe you have a touch of 'flu!' You realise that she is (as always) right, and the internal mechanism suddenly lets go, muttering, 'All right! Give it the works! You can be as sick as you like—until Sunday midnight.'' Away you stagger, hardly able to stand upright. You retire to bed with a hot whisky and lemon. Your temperature reaches 102° that night and you wonder whether you have a fifty-fifty chance of survival. None can be so desperately ill as those whose general health is excellent. By Saturday midday you send for your solicitor (who can't be found, having gone fishing), saying that you must alter your will—a matter of some small bequest to a medical research foundation. By Saturday night you are on the point of death. On Sunday morning you are recovering. During the afternoon you are convalescent. And by Monday morning you are back at your desk and perfectly well. The existence or absence of this internal mechanism is a simple question of fact. If you don't have it, you are not of the stuff of which Numbers One are made. You have it? Yes? Then go on to the next question.

QUESTION TWO: *Are you prepared to do whatever the other fellows can't or won't?* In theory, everyone on the pay-roll is there to do what he or she is told. In practice, however, they do as they like. One has a taste for public relations and another likes to file documents where they can never again be found. One loves to draw up organisation charts and another goes round switching off the lights. But there is one man who cannot do what he likes and that is Number One. For on him devolves, in addition to his normal work, the job that is left over; and no one can guess what that is going to be. It may be working out the vacation roster or it may be choosing the paint. It might be checking the gas consumption and then again it might be testing the fire drill. It could be having the windows cleaned or it could be mending the fuse. But whatever it may chance to be, there is nobody left to do it—except Number One. It is what no one else will do that falls, in the end, to him. Are you prepared for this and cheerfully confident? You are? Then go on to the last question—which is not so easy.

QUESTION THREE: *Are you prepared to sack Joe Wittering?* You know him, of course. Every organisation has or has had a Joe Wittering. He is quite honest and very generally liked and is one of the most well-meaning fellows alive. He bumbles around harmlessly with unanswered letters in his pocket, breakfast smears on his tie, cigarette ash on his trousers, and a vacant smile on his face. Joe is known to everybody as a kindly old muddler with a popular wife and five children at school. There might be a case

113

for retaining Joe but we'll suppose that there isn't. In another organisation he might have been useful, even invaluable, as the man who is always wrong. But times are hard, competition is keen, money is scarce, and we can't afford to make any more mistakes. Joe has to be fired. As Number One, it is your job and no one else's to send for Joe and say: 'You are not good enough for this company and I am abolishing your post as from October 1st. You have until then to find yourself another job. Short of perjury, I shall do what I can for you.' His face will go white and his hands will tremble. He will stammer something about his past work, about his wife and kids, to which you will reply: 'I'm sorry, Joe, but my decision is final.' You are ready to do that? But this is not the whole of the test. For, having looked Joe Wittering in the eyes and said 'You're sacked,' you have to go home and sleep soundly, not having given the matter another thought.

To be a good Number Two (which you are) you need knowledge, skill, ability, and tact. All these you need as Number One but with something else, that touch of ruthlessness which distinguishes the man at the top. It may be a general's duty to order the blowing of a bridge, knowing that some of his own troops are still on the other side. It may fall to a ship's commander to close the watertight bulkhead, with stokers trapped beyond. Nor is this sort of decision taken with cinematic emotion. It is done calmly and coldly, leaving only that permanently changed expression of the mouth and the eyes. Do you pass that final test in its lesser peacetime form? It is not merely a question, remember, of sacking Joe Wittering. You must sleep soundly afterwards. There must be no wondering 'Did I do the right thing?', no guesses as to what the Witterings will do, but an instant switching to the next problem; which may indeed be the sacking of somebody else.

We shall suppose now that you have given the right answers to each of the three vital questions. All your ailments happen between Friday afternoon and Monday morning. You are able and ready to do whatever job is left over. And you are prepared to sack Joe Wittering. With all your experience and ability and with the three additional qualities that mark you out for leadership, you have nevertheless been turned down. With a barely credible want of common sense, the Board have appointed a younger man as chief, leaving you as Number Two. Human failings being what they are, this sad fate could befall anyone; and so, after years of successful work, it has happened to you. The new Number One has arrived and you have bid him welcome on behalf of the salaried staff. You have added your own warm congratulations, noting inwardly that his hair is thinning and that his suit is badly tailored. Your wife considers that Number One's wife is older than she pretends to be and that her taste in dress is almost (well, let's face it) *dowdy*. The ceremonies are over and now the question is—what are you to do next?

Until very recently there would have been no answer to this question. The only hope for Number Two, we should have had to admit, lies in the possibility of Number One having a long and serious illness, leaving Number Two well established by the time Number One actually resigns or dies. But this sort of illness is, in fact, extremely unlikely. In the words of the proverb, a watched pot never boils. The person who is to benefit from an annuity will live forever. It is no good waiting for Number One to fall sick. The better policy is to manœuvre him out of the

way. It is widely believed that people can be forced to
retire by a combination of form-filling and air-travel. So
they can (see *infra*, pages 129 and 135). Well-tried methods
sometimes fail. Nor will this surprise anyone who has ever
used insecticide. In the first years, as we know, an insecticide
will produce some results; not killing the mosquitoes,
perhaps, but definitely giving them the sense of being
unwanted. In the second year their feelings are unhurt—
they are used to it. In the third year they like it. And in the
fourth year they quite possibly cannot live without it. So it
is with some high executives. They have come to look
upon aircraft with a tolerance bordering on affection. So
the need arises for some other means of discouraging those
senior to us. It is just such a secret that is now to be
revealed.

This most Up-to-Date form of Number-One-Removal
involves the application of Management Science. If you,
as Number Two, are unfamiliar with Management Science,
your first move should be to hire a Ph.D from, say,
Manchester. Experts in this field are numerous and cheap,
so that there should be no difficulty in recruiting a
Management Scientist from a Business School. Suppose
that the one chosen is Dr. Hellkite, whose wife is herself
a known specialist in Behaviour. You persuade Number
One to allow the Head Office to be made the subject
of a technical investigation. The whole programme will
be at the expense (you will explain) of the Hecate
Institute, which has provided three research assistants.
And now the staff meeting is to receive the first Interim
Report.

DUNCAN: Item 3. Report from Dr Hellkite, copies of
which have been circulated. Any comments?

CAREERS

MACBETH: I suggest, sir, that we invite Dr Hellkite to explain his project. Here he is. . . .

DUNCAN: Very well, Number Two. Dr Hellkite, the floor is yours.

HELLKITE: My object, gentlemen, is to present our Interim Report in the simplest form. The facts already revealed call for immediate action. To wait for the final report would be to let the situation deteriorate. Briefly, then, I have made a preliminary study of this organisation, using Batworthy's non-linear extension of the optimal range. . . .

MACBETH: With internal validity checks, I hope?

HELLKITE: Certainly. You will find a note on diagnostic procedures at Appendix K. Applying a strategy of random variables and using the Stochastic Model; applying, moreover, our experience of operations research and decision theory, we could not escape the meaningful conclusion which we have tabulated on pages 34 to 37.

DUNCAN: Very interesting, but I really don't see . . .

MACBETH: Forgive my interrupting, sir, but I think I can explain the passage which you find obscure. I was puzzled myself and asked Dr Hellkite why he rejected the simpler strategy of Filkenstein's Theorem. But he soon convinced me that quadratic programming would not, in this case, have been helpful. I think you will find the report in other respects both lucid and cogent.

Pause now and reflect, for the staff meeting has reached what is known in the bullfighting arena as the Moment of Truth. For Number One it is a question of Now or Never. To regain control of the situation he must at this point drop his copy of the Interim Report into the wastepaper basket and address Dr Hellkite in some such words as these:

DUNCAN: All this sounds to me like froth and gas. I haven't the least idea what you are talking about and have no reason to think that it matters. If you have any constructive comments to make on our organisation, make them in plain language, stating what you think should be done. But don't talk to me as you might to a digital computer. I don't like it, don't grasp it, and won't have it.

By this brusque reaction, which will reduce Dr Hellkite to a twittering ineptitude, Number One can defeat the whole plot. In a moment all those present will be admitting in chorus that the Interim Report is so much meaningless drivel. The founder of the company, old Tom Tuffenuff, would have done exactly that. But today's executives are seldom men of his calibre. It takes some courage to profess a scornful ignorance among a whole group of executives, each professing to follow the whole argument. In nine cases out of ten, Number One will fail the test. He will nod his head in feigned comprehension. And once the moment has passed, he will never regain control of the meeting, which will continue on these lines:

DUNCAN: Thank you, Mac. The Report might have been worded more clearly, but I think we all understand the Doctor's point. (*He looks round.*)

ALL (*Quickly*): Yes, yes. Perfectly clear.

MACBETH: Well, I seem to be the dunce here, but I'm still puzzled by the last half of page 41. Why should dynamic programming involve the theory of games?

HELLKITE: I'm glad you asked that. My symbol manipulation language is not as coherent as it should be. The page summarises my heuristic line-balancing procedure, which leads to the non-basic optimum solution on the next page.

MACBETH: But that solution is inconsistent, surely, with the combinational analysis and topology on page 17—look, you say here that

$$II = \frac{1}{mm} - (p + h^2)$$

What about the calculus of probabilities?

HELLKITE: It doesn't apply to a multiperson interaction. It *would* have applied, I freely admit, had I been using a different methodology. But the conclusions would have been much the same.

MACBETH: Oh, I'm not questioning that. The Zoning-Constraint would not have been affected.

HELLKITE: Exactly! It is a question of cybernetics and a use of the minimax principle. We are basically in agreement, I think.

MACBETH: That is so. But your exhaustive algorithms leave me with a regret function which defies analysis.

HELLKITE (*Laughing heartily*): Good, good!

ALL (*Smiling nervously*): He, he, he. . .

MACBETH: Well, sir. We have, as I see it, to apply this Report to the Activation of Motives in our organisation. I suggest, however, that we defer action until Part II of the final report is before us, which will be in about three weeks' time. The matter can wait until then, I imagine, but not much longer—isn't that right?

HELLKITE: We need a firm decision before the end of the month.

MACBETH: Right. And we shall need to discuss Part II at some length before we outline our programme.

DUNCAN (*Apprehensively*): At some length?

MACBETH: Well, we need to know what we are doing.

DUNCAN: (*Crushed*): I suppose so. . . .

MACBETH: And I feel we should thank Dr Hellkite for all his help.

ALL: Yes, yes. Very valuable indeed.

HELLKITE: I could never have produced this Interim Report without the help of the three research assistants provided for me by the Hecate Institute. Miss Weard and her two sisters have done a fine job. Might I convey to them the Company's thanks?

DUNCAN: I suppose so.

HELLKITE: They will greatly appreciate it.

DUNCAN: And now, Dr Hellkite, you will be wanting to get back to your investigations. Thank you, Doctor. . . . Now—Item 4. The estimate for repairing the powerhouse roof. Mr Macduff?

Number One will bluster over Item 4 but he has nevertheless lost ground. By next week he will have to face another discussion with Dr Hellkite and still without the least idea of what is to be discussed. Then will come the final report. In this Dr Hellkite will include his masterpiece, the Model to illustrate the Head Office Social System. As this represents the last deadly stroke, it is worth reproducing in full—see overleaf.

At the sight of this diagram, Number One will utter a hollow groan. 'Oh, *no*!' he will whisper, 'not *that*!' But *that* is nevertheless what he has to face. All he can do is to retire to bed with a migraine, leaving Number Two to carry out the planned reorganisation. Whenever Number One shows signs of recovery, a mere flourish of this diagram, a mere distant echo of Dr Hellkite's voice, will be enough to bring on a relapse. The time for Number One's retirement is near and there can be no doubt as to who his successor must be. Nor is there any doubt as to what you do with Dr Hellkite as soon as the farewells have been said. 'Out!' you will say briefly, proving once more

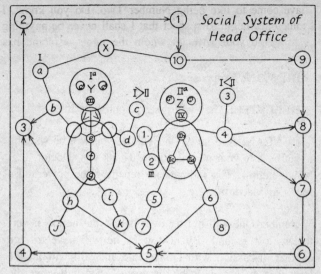

Social System of Head Office

that the hired assassin becomes unwelcome after the deed has been done. Do you hesitate to use this method of removing Number One? Do you recoil from treating any man with such calculated cruelty? If so, the feeling does you credit. You have a loftier moral code and higher ethical principles than many a minister of religion. You have all the selfless motivation which may fit you for the second post in any organisation; and there, as Number Two, you are likely to remain. For the Numbers One of this world are ultimately ruthless. They will use any means to gain their end, and if Management Science looks usefully lethal, that is the weapon they will use. Shrink from this nebulous dagger and you will soon be thinking (and quite rightly, from your point of view) that to be Number One is hardly worth the pain and effort. One day, by your fireside, with pipe lit and coffee at your elbow, you will say to your wife, 'Ambition is all very well . . . but I have come to like being Number Two. Do you know, I sometimes begin to suspect that I shall never be anything else?' And your wife, to whom the same suspicion has been a certainty for the last six years, will calmly and smilingly agree.

9

Pension Point
or Age of Retirement

To the many problems we have been discussing we should now add the question of retirement. It has been the subject of many commissions of inquiry but the evidence heard has always been hopelessly conflicting and the final recommendations muddled, inconclusive, and vague. Ages of compulsory retirement are fixed at points varying from 55 to 75, all being equally arbitrary and unscientific. Whatever age has been decreed by accident and custom can be defended by the same argument. Where the retirement age is fixed at 65 the defenders of this system will always have found, by experience, that the mental powers and energy show signs of flagging at the age of 62. This would be a most useful conclusion to have reached had not a different phenomenon been observed in organisations where the age of retirement has been fixed at 60. There, we are told, people are found to lose their grip, in some degree, at the age of 57. As against that, men whose retiring age is 55 are known to be past their best at 52. It would seem, in short, that efficiency declines at the age of R minus 3, irrespective of the age at which R has been fixed. This is an interesting fact in itself but not directly helpful when it comes to deciding what the R age is to be.

But while the R − 3 age is not directly useful to us, it may serve to suggest that the investigations hitherto pursued have been on the wrong lines. The observation often made that men vary, some being old at 50, others still energetic at 80 or 90, may well be true, but here again the fact leads us nowhere. The truth is that the age of retirement should not be related in any way to the man whose retirement we are considering. It is his successor we have to watch: the man (Y) destined to replace the other man (X) when the latter retires. He will pass, as is well known, the following stages in his successful career:

1	Age of Qualification	(Q)	
2	Age of Discretion	(D)	= Q + 3
3	Age of Promotion	(P)	= D + 7
4	Age of Responsibility	(R)	= P + 5
5	Age of Authority	(A)	= R + 3
6	Age of Achievement	(AA)	= A + 7
7	Age of Distinction	(DD)	= AA + 9
8	Age of Dignity	(DDD)	= DD + 6
9	Age of Wisdom	(W)	= DDD + 3
10	Age of Obstruction	(OO)	= W + 7

The above scale is governed by the numerical value of Q. Now, Q is to be understood as a technical term. It does not mean that a man at Q knows anything of the business he will have to transact. Architects, for example, pass some form of examinations but are seldom found to know anything useful at that point (or indeed any other point) in their career. The term Q means the age at which a professional or business career begins, usually after an elaborate training that has proved profitable only to those paid for organising it. It will be seen that if $Q = 22$, X will not reach OO (the Age of Obstruction) until he is 72. So far as his own efficiency is concerned, there is no valid reason for replacing him until he is 71. But our problem centres not on him but on Y, his destined successor. How are the ages of X and Y likely to compare? To be more exact, how old will X have been when Y first entered the department or firm?

This problem has been the subject of prolonged investigation. Our inquiries have tended to prove that the age gap between X and Y is exactly fifteen years. (It is not, we find, the normal practice for the son to succeed the father directly.) Taking this average of fifteen years, and assuming that $Q = 22$, we find that Y will have reached AA (the Age of Achievement) at 47, when X is only 62. And that, clearly, is where the crisis occurs. For Y, if thwarted in his ambition through X's still retaining control, enters, it has been proved, an alternative sequence in his career. These stages (after 5) are as follows:

6	Age of Frustration	(F)	=	$A + 7$
7	Age of Jealousy	(J)	=	$F + 9$
8	Age of Resignation	(R)	=	$J + 4$
9	Age of Oblivion	(O)	=	$R + 5$

When X, therefore, is 72, Y is 57, just entering into the Age of Resignation. Should X at last retire at that age. Y is quite unfit to take his place, being now resigned (after a decade of frustration and jealousy) to a career of mediocrity. For Y, opportunity will have come just ten years too late.

The Age of Frustration will not always be the same in years, depending as it does on the factor Q, but its symptoms are easy to recognise. The man who is denied the opportunity of taking decisions of importance begins to regard as important the decisions he is allowed to take. He becomes fussy about filing, keen on seeing that pencils are sharpened, eager to ensure that the windows are open (or shut), and apt to use two or three different coloured inks. The Age of Jealousy reveals itself in an emphasis upon seniority. 'After all, I am still somebody.' 'I was never consulted.' 'Z has very little experience.' But that period gives place to the Age of Resignation. 'I am not one of these ambitious types.' 'Z is welcome to a seat on the Board—more trouble than it is worth, I should say.' 'Promotion would only have interfered with my golf.' The theory has been advanced that the Age of Frustration is also marked by an interest in local politics. It is now known, however, that men enter local politics partly as a result of being unhappily married. It will be apparent, however, from the other symptoms described, that the man still in a subordinate position at 47 (or equivalent) will never be fit for anything else.

The problem, it is now clear, is to make X retire at the age of 60, while still able to do the work better than anyone else. The immediate change may be for the worse but the alternative is to have no possible successor at hand when X finally goes. And the more outstanding X has proved to be, and the longer his period of office, the more hopeless is the task of replacing him. Those nearest him in seniority are already too old and have been subordinate for too long. All they can do is to block the way for anyone junior to them; a task in which they will certainly not fail. No competent successor will appear for years, nor at all until some crisis has brought a new leader to the fore. So the hard decision has to be taken. Unless X goes in good time, the whole organisation will eventually suffer. But how is X to be removed?

In this, as in so many other matters, modern science is not at a loss. The crude methods of the past have been superseded. In days gone by it was usual, no doubt, for the other directors to talk inaudibly at board meetings, one merely opening and shutting his mouth and another nodding in apparent comprehension, thus convincing the chairman that he was actually going deaf. But there is a modern technique that is far more effective and certain. The method depends essentially on air travel and filling in of forms. Research has shown that complete exhaustion in modern life results from a combination of these two activities. The high official who is given enough of each will very soon begin to talk of retirement. It used to be the custom in primitive tribal groups to liquidate the king or chief at a certain point in his career, either after a period of years or at the moment when his vital powers appeared to have gone. Nowadays the technique is to lay before the great man the programme of a conference at Helsinki in June, a congress at Adelaide in July, and a convention at Ottawa in August, each lasting about three weeks. He is assured that the prestige of the department or firm will depend on his presence and that the delegation of this duty to anyone else would be regarded as an insult by all others taking part. The programme of travel will allow of his return to the office for about three or four days between one conference and the next. He will find his in-tray piled high on each occasion with forms to fill in, some relating to his travels, some to do with applications for permits or quota allocations, and the rest headed 'Income Tax.' On his completion of the forms awaiting his signature after the Ottawa convention, he will be given the programme for a new series of conferences; one at Manila in September, the second at Mexico City in October, and the third at Quebec in November. By December he will admit that he is feeling his age. In January he will announce his intention to retire.

The essence of this technique is so to arrange matters that the conferences are held at places the maximum distance apart and in climates offering the sharpest contrast in heat and cold. There should be no possibility whatever of a restful sea voyage in any part of the schedule. It must be air travel all the way. No particular care need be taken in the choice between one route and another. All are alike in being planned for the convenience of the mails rather than the passengers. It can safely be assumed, almost without inquiry, that most flights will involve take-offs at 2:50 a.m., reporting at the airfield at 1:30 and weighing baggage at the terminal at 12:45. Arrival will be scheduled for 3:10 a.m. on the next day but one. The aircraft will invariably, however, be somewhat overdue, touching down in fact at 3:57 a.m., so that passengers will be clear of customs and immigration by about 4:35. Going one way around the world, it is possible and indeed customary to have breakfast about three times. In the opposite direction the passengers will have nothing to eat for hours at a stretch, being finally offered a glass of sherry when on the point of collapse from malnutrition. Most of the flight time will of course be spent in filling in various declarations about currency and health. How much have you in dollars (U.S.), pounds (sterling), francs, marks, guilders, yen, lire, and pounds (Australian); how much in letters of credit, travellers' cheques, postage stamps, and postal orders?' Where did you sleep last night and the night before that? (This last is an easy question, for the air traveller is usually able to declare, in good faith, that he has not slept at all

130

for the past week.) When were you born and what was your grandmother's maiden name? How many children have you and why? What will be the length of your stay and where? What is the object of your visit, if any? (As if by now you could even remember.) Have you had chicken-pox and why not? Have you a visa for Patagonia and a re-entry permit for Hong Kong? The penalty for making a false declaration is life imprisonment. Fasten your seat belts, please. We are about to land at Rangoon. Local time is 2:47 a.m. Outside temperature is 110° F. We shall stop here for approximately one hour. Breakfast will be served on the aircraft five hours after take-off. Thank you. (For what, in heaven's name?) No smoking, please.

It will be observed that air travel, considered as a retirement-accelerator, has the advantage of including a fair amount of form-filling. But form-filling proper is a separate ordeal, not necessarily connected with travel. The

art of devising forms to be filled in depends on three elements: obscurity, lack of space, and the heaviest penalties for failure. In a form-compiling department, obscurity is ensured by various branches dealing respectively with ambiguity, irrelevance, and jargon. But some of the simpler devices have now become automatic. Thus, a favourite opening gambit is a section, usually in the top right-hand corner, worded thus:

Return rendered in respect of the month of	

As you have been sent the form on 16 February, you have no idea whether it relates to last month, this month, or next. Only the sender knows that, but he is asking you. At this point the ambiguity expert takes over, collaborating closely with a space consultant, and this is the result:

Cross out the word which does not apply	Full name	Address	Domicile	When naturalised and why	Status
Mr Mrs Miss					

Such a form as this is especially designed, of course, for a Colonel, Lord, Professor, or Doctor called Alexander Winthrop Percival Blenkinsop-Fotheringay of Battleaxe Towers, Layer-de-la-Haye, near Newcastle-under-Lyme, Lincolnshire-parts-of-Kesteven (whatever that may mean). Follows the word 'Domicile,' which is practically meaningless except to an international lawyer, and after that a mysterious reference to naturalisation. Lastly, we have the word 'Status,' which leaves the filler-in wondering whether to put 'Admiral (Retd.),' 'Married,' 'American Citizen,' or 'Managing Director.'

Now the ambiguity expert hands over the task to a specialist in irrelevance, who calls in a new space allocator to advise on layout:

Number of your identity card or passport	Your grand-father's full name	Your grand-mother's maiden name	Have you been vaccinated, inoculated; when & why	Give full details

Note: The penalty for furnishing incorrect information may be a fine of £5,000 or a year's penal servitude, or quite possibly both.

Then the half-completed work of art is sent to the jargon specialist, who produces something on these lines:

What special circumstances[253] are alleged to justify the adjusted allocation for which request is made in respect of the quota period to which the former applications[143] relates, whether or not the former level had been revised and in what sense and for what purpose and whether this or any previous application made by any other party or parties has been rejected by any other planning authority under subsection VII[35] or for any other reason, and whether this or the latter decision was made the subject of any appeal and with what result and why.

Finally, the form goes to the technician, who adds the space-for-signature section, the finish that crowns the whole.

I/we [block capitals]. . . . . .declare under penalty that all the information I/we have furnished above is true to the best of my/our knowledge, as witness my/our signature signed this. . . . . . day of. . . . . . . .19. . . . ,

   (Signature). . . . .
WITNESS:

	Photograph Passport Size	Seal. . . . .
Name.		
Address.		*Thumb*
Occupation.		*Print*

This is quite straightforward except for the final touch of confusion as to whose photograph or thumb print is wanted, the I/we person or the witness. It probably does not matter, anyway.

Experiment has shown that an elderly man in a responsible position will soon be forced to retire if given sufficient air travel and sufficient forms. Instances are frequent, moreover, of such elderly men deciding to retire before the treatment has even begun. At the first mention of a conference at Stockholm or Vancouver, they often realise that their time has arrived. Very rarely nowadays is it necessary to adopt methods of a severe character. The last recorded resort to these was in a period soon after the conclusion of World War II. The high official concerned was particularly tough and the only remedy found was to send him on a tour of tin mines and rubber estates in Malaya. This method is best tried in January, and with jet aircraft to make the climatic transition more abrupt. On landing at 5:52 p.m.

(Malayan time) this official was rushed off at once to a cocktail party, from that to another cocktail party (held at a house fifteen miles from the hotel where the first took place), and from that to a dinner party (eleven miles in the opposite direction). He was in bed by about 2:30 a.m. and on board an aircraft at seven the next morning. Landing at Ipoh for a belated breakfast, he was then taken to visit two rubber estates, a tin mine, an oil-palm plantation, and a factory for canning pineapples. After lunch, given by the Rotary Club, he was taken to a school, a clinic, and a community centre. There followed two cocktail parties and a Chinese banquet of twenty courses, the numerous toasts being drunk in neat brandy served in tumblers. The formal discussion on policy began next morning and lasted for three days, the meetings interspersed with formal receptions and nightly banquets in Sumatran or Indian style. That the treatment was too severe was fairly apparent by the fifth day, during the afternoon of which the distinguished visitor could walk only when supported by a secretary on one side, a personal assistant on the other. On the sixth day he died, thus confirming the general impression that he must have been tired or unwell. Such methods as these are now discountenanced, and have since indeed proved needless. People are learning to retire in time.

But a serious problem remains. What are we ourselves to do when nearing the retirement age we have fixed for others? It will be obvious at once that our own case is entirely different from any other case we have so far considered. We do not claim to be outstanding in any way, but it just so happens that there is no possible successor in sight. It is with genuine reluctance that we agree to postpone our retirement for a few years, purely in the public interest. And when a senior member of the staff approaches us with details of a conference at Stockholm or Hobart, we promptly wave it aside, announcing that all conferences are a waste of time. 'Besides,' we continue blandly, 'my arrangements are already made. I shall be salmon fishing for the next two months and will return to this office at the end of October, by which date I shall expect all the forms to have been filled in. Good-bye until then.' We knew how to make our predecessors retire. When it comes to forcing our own retirement, our successors must find some method of their own.

TACTICS

10

Abominable No-Man
or Abandon Hope

MANY OF THE BASIC CONCEPTS IN PUBLIC AND BUSINESS administration were first defined by Dr P. G. Wodehouse, but they are now so much a part of contemporary thought that their origin is often forgotten. No one can now recall a time when Yes-men and Nodders were not sharply differentiated in the textbooks, but seldom is credit for this useful distinction given to the thinker who first perceived wherein the difference lies. Among the few, however, who remember Wodehouse's first brilliant paper (read before the Royal Society in 1929) there is a feeling of regret that his attention was never drawn to the opposite sub-species: the No-men and the Shakers. One reason why his researches stopped where they did is that Yes-men operate *within* an organisation while No-men are more prominent in its external relations. It may seem presumptuous to draw distinctions where so great a scientist as Wodehouse could perceive none, but there is no doubt that some classifying and defining would be at least convenient, even if we recognise, as we must, that it cannot be final. Recent research has shown that administrative organisations, whether governmental or industrial, have two vertical channels. There is, on the one hand, the channel through which the decisions taken on the highest level are filtered down to the pyramid's base. There is, on the other hand, the channel through which applications, suggestions, and appeals make their way from the base to the summit. These two channels seldom correspond to those which exist on paper but research has shown that the chain of command on the executive side goes from the Chief to the Knowman and so to the Yes-men (Senior and Junior) and at last to the Nodders. The theory has been propounded that the incoming proposal is dealt with on the contemplative side by the Shakers, the No-men (Senior and Junior) and the Don't-knowmen and, eventually, the Chief. There are two objections to this theory, however; in the first place, it does not tally with our experience. In the second place, it does not explain how any idea ever reaches the Chief at all. The truth is that the contemplative side of an organisation is seldom entirely negative. What we actually find is that two types alternate at different levels. We thus find the Admirable Willingman alternating with the Abominable No-man. We find that Nodders intermingle with the Shakers.

To the man outside the hierarchy with an idea to sell, the effect is one of alternating despair and hope; an effect best to be described in narrative form. Picture, to begin with, the head office or Ministry. Beneath the visitor's left arm is the scheme, the plan, the blueprint, or brainwave. Trembling slightly, he is shown into the office of Mr Jolly D. Goodfellow, who wears country tweeds and an Old Receptonian tie.

'Come in, Mr Hopefall. Take the armchair. Do you smoke? Forgive me a moment while I send for your file. Valerie, would you mind bringing the file on the Hopefall Project? I had it yesterday. . . . Ah, here it is! Thank you, Monica: you look very glamorous today—a lunch engagement? All right, we shan't expect you back until three-ish. . . . Now, here is the file, right up to date. I have studied your scheme very carefully and can see no objection to it. In fact, I think it most ingenious. We should all congratulate you on the method by which you propose to overcome the main technical difficulty. A neat solution, lucidly explained! The scheme has my fullest support.'

'We can go ahead, then?' asks Mr Hopefall, scarcely able to believe his ears.

'Yes, yes, certainly!'

'What—now?'

'Yes, immediately. Well, *almost* immediately. As soon as we have the Chief's signature. I foresee no difficulty of any kind.'

'You can't approve it yourself?'

'Well, no, not exactly. But I can advise the Deputy Assistant. *He* can approve it straight away; and I expect he will.'

'That is terribly kind of you.'

'Not in the least. We are here to serve the public, I always say; not to create difficulties just for the love of obstruction. We are definitely out to help all we can. That is our job. . . . Now, I have added my strong recommendation on the minute sheet. All I need do now is sign it—so. And we might do well to accelerate the process a bit. Valerie, do be a dear and find me an URGENT label in red. Thank you, that's fine. See that this file goes *direct* to the Deputy Assistant. Come back tomorrow at this time, Mr Hopefall, and you should be able to go ahead on the following day. Ask for me personally and telephone extension 374 if you have the least difficulty. It has been a pleasure meeting you, Mr Hopefall. Goodbye for the present, and all good luck with your project. You have nothing further to worry about.'

On the next day, Hopefall is told that the Deputy Assistant can see him at 12:30. After waiting in the outer office, he is shown at 1:45 into the small bare room occupied by Mr Ivor Snagge, who wears deep mourning, rimless spectacles, and a shifty expression.

'Ah, Mr Hopefall, I have been studying this scheme of yours. . . .'

'I trust my memorandum sets it out adequately. If there is anything I can explain more clearly, I shall be glad to do so.'

'That won't be necessary. The proposal is clearly described. The trouble is—(Miss Tightlace—shut the window, please. There's a draught!)—What was I saying? Ah, yes. The trouble is that the scheme is impracticable, unacceptable, and quite possibly illegal. It is, to my mind, *completely* out of the question.'

'Oh, but *why*?'

'Completely and utterly impossible. I should have thought that even Goodfellow would have realised that. On financial grounds alone.'

'But, surely—'

'Out of the question, Mr Horsfall. The objections to the plan are as numerous as they are insuperable. (Miss Tightlace—wedge some paper under that window—I can *still* feel a draught.) No, Mr Horsfall, it cannot be done.'

'Are you sure that you have the right file before you? My name is not Horsfall but Hopefall.'

'So you think I would deal with a matter of this kind without studying the right file?'

'Well, you hadn't the right name.'

'And that proves that our whole procedure is careless, haphazard, and lax?'

'I never said that.'

'I think you did.'

'In that case you are prejudiced against me and should refer the matter to higher authority.'

'That is what I intend to do. In the meanwhile, I must ask you to leave this office before I send for the police. No violence, please! Your application is rejected. That is final, and you will gain nothing by abusive language. Good-day to you, Sir.'

*   *   *

Ten days later Mr Hopefall will be edging nervously into the presence of the Assistant Director, wondering what to expect this time. He need not have worried, however, for Mr O. H. Gladleigh is both helpful and charming.

'I have a minute here from Snagge but we won't take that too seriously. I expect you saw him about lunch time. A most conscientious worker, you know, but a bit testy after midday. Now, about your proposed scheme, I can see no real objection to it. In principle it should be accepted. I only wish I could do that at once on my own authority. In view, however, of the points raised by Snagge, I think it will have to go to the Deputy Director. I shall strongly advise him to authorise the scheme, treating the matter as one of high priority.'

A week later Mr Hopefall will march confidently into the Deputy Director's office, to be confronted by a tall, thin man of haggard appearance staring hopelessly into some dreadful futurity. This is Mr Longstop. He holds the file limply and motions his visitor to a chair. There is a silence of a minute or two, and then Mr Longstop sighs 'No.' After another minute he utters, 'Can't be done. . . .' Then at last he asks:

'Have you considered all the difficulties? Financial? Political? Economic? Have you assessed the probable reaction overseas? Have you tried to judge what the effect will be on the United Nations? I am sorry, Mr Hopefall, but I have no alternative. What you propose is, frankly, impossible.'

*   *   *

He will end by referring the matter again to higher authority. Nor need we follow the file to its logical conclusion. It is already apparent that the Admirable Willingmen alternate in sequence with the Abominable No-men. The final decision must depend, therefore, upon the number of levels in the organisation or (to be more exact) upon the relative position of the level at which the decision will be made.

From a study of this administrative behaviour pattern it is possible to lay down certain principles to be observed by those who approach the organisation. The first rule, clearly, is to persist. The applicant who left the building for ever after an interview with Snagge or Longstop would never have met Mr Gladleigh nor spoken with Longstop's superior, Mr O. K. Oldmann. The best policy, it must be obvious, is to presevere until you find a Willingman.

The situation is one that we often encounter when shopping. The assistant says at once, 'No, we have no Sopvite Shaving Cream. There is very little demand for it.' The experienced customer perceives at once that the assistant is too lazy to see whether he/she has the stuff or not. He decides, therefore, to wait. He finds a stool and settles down with an air of limitless patience. In ten minutes the assistant, sick of the sight of him, produces the Sopvite, muttering that he/she has found an old tube left over. He/she will have had to arrange for the opening of a new crate but there is no need to comment upon this. The point is that persistence has won. In the imaginary examples quoted the various executives have automatically referred the proposal each time to higher authority. In real life they might not have done this. The technique, therefore, is to sit patiently until they do. It is needless to say anything much. Just sit and stare at the executive until exasperation forces his hand. Inclination and habit will alike induce him to refer the matter to someone else. You will then have scored a point, for the other man can hardly be more obstructive and may well be less.

The second rule is to make use of the Willingman when you have found him. Your object this time is to obtain a decision and prevent reference to the next higher level. You will know from experience that a Willingman's superior is normally a No-man. You must, therefore, convince the Willingman that the decision can be his. The technique should be one of regret that so trifling a matter should have been allowed to reach so senior an executive.

'I am really ashamed,' you will repeat, 'that your time should be occupied in this way. It is satisfactory for me, I will admit, to discuss the question with a man actually responsible for making big decisions. One tires of argument with mere underlings. But this problem scarcely deserves your notice.'

Expanding in the warmth of your admiration, the Willingman may quite possibly sign his approval there and then, irrevocably committing his superiors to a policy of which they know nothing; and this is exactly what you want.

The third rule is to avoid wasting time on the No-man once he has been identified. It is a common error to suppose that the No-man could be convinced by argument and might eventually say 'Yes.' But that is to misunderstand the No-man's character. His automatic negative does not arise from any rational opposition to your scheme as such. He says 'No' because he has found that this is the easiest way and because he never says anything else. Should he say 'Yes' he might be asked to explain the basis for his enthusiasm. Should he approve, he might be involved in work resulting from the proposal's acceptance. Should the scheme prove a failure he might be held responsible for advocating it in the first place. But saying 'No' is relatively safe. It requires no explanation because those higher in the organisation need never know that the proposal was ever received. It involves no work because no action follows. Nor can the scheme fail for it will not even be tried. The only danger is that the applicant may gain a hearing some other way; but even later acceptance of the plan need not worry the No-man unduly. He cannot be held responsible for any failure and will not be asked to aid in ensuring success. Few will remember his opposition and those who do can be told that the plan *in its original form* was impracticable and that its effective application, after revision, owed much to the process of healthy criticism to which it was subjected in the early stages of its development. The No-man has little to lose.

The successful application of the principles here revealed depends not upon argument as to the merits of the case but upon a preliminary survey of the organisation. The correct procedure is to count the number of levels and discover where the No-men are placed. Make a chart of the whole structure indicating the No-men as so many black squares in what we can fairly describe as the crossword puzzle. Then plan your campaign so as to avoid the black squares, side-stepping from one Willingman to the next, and so reaching the lowest level at which a decision is possible. In an organisation comprising executives who always say 'Yes,' and executives who always say 'No,' the problem is not one of argument but of pattern. The navigator does not argue with rocks; he avoids them. That this is the right policy is apparent to anyone who knows that the rocks (the No-men) exist. As against that, it would be wrong to imagine that these elementary principles comprise the whole of knowledge. The problem of nomanity, as here defined or at least described, awaits detailed investigation. Our researches have scarcely begun.

11

Law of Delay
or Playing for Time

THERE IS NOTHING STATIC IN OUR CHANGING WORLD
and recent research has tended to show that the Abominable No-man is being replaced by the Prohibitive Procrastinator. Instead of saying 'No' the PP says 'In due course'
(scientifically, IDC), these words foreshadowing Negation
by Delay (scientifically, ND). The theory of ND depends
upon establishing a rough idea of what amount of delay
will equal negation. If we suppose that a drowning man
calls for help, evoking the reply 'In due course,' a judicious pause of five minutes may constitute for all practical
purposes, a negative response. Why? Because the delay is
greater than the non-swimmer's expectation of life. The
same principal holds good in a case at law. A, divorced
from B, demands the custody of their daughter (aged 17)
but is told by counsel that she will be of age before the
case can be determined. At the retail level, A is told by his
ironmonger, B, that the lawnmower he wants can be deliv-

ered in six months (i.e., by December). All these are examples of ND in its simpler forms.

Where the urgent matter requires remedial legislation, delay takes on a new dimension. The judicious pause will correspond, nevertheless, to the life-expectation of the man from whom the proposal originates. If it is the divorce laws which obviously need revision, the Prohibitive Procrastinator starts by asking about the age and health of the Reformer whose Bill it is. Taking the age of 70 as the basis of his calculation, modified by actuarial factors, he concludes that Reformer A may expect to agitate for another eight years. Negation by Delay (ND) means the process of ensuring that 'in due course' (IDC) will mean, in this instance, nine years from now. Realisation that the IDC is greater than the Reformer's expected life of agitation (LA) is often enough to kill the whole idea at the outset. For many altruistic men the knowledge that it cannot be done in their lifetime is equivalent to the knowledge that it cannot be done at all. Where a useful reform takes place, as must occasionally happen, this is the result of the Reformer's living and working for years beyond the limits of reasonable expectation. The Reformer may thus outlive the PP, whose especial hatred is of reformers much younger than himself. There are cases, therefore, where the IDC factor is less than the LA and some half-hearted legislation is the result. But men like Sir Alan Herbert have never been numerous and they are tending, in fact, to become extinct. The average reformer or innovator gives up more easily, leaving the PP in a position of strength, ready to defeat the next proposal by using the same technique. Delays are thus deliberately designed as a form of denial and are extended to cover the life expectation of the person whose proposal is being pigeon-holed. DELAY IS THE DEADLIEST FORM OF DENIAL. This is the Law of Delay. In mathematical terms it is represented by the equation:

Where

L = LA or the expected life of the person from whom the proposed reform originates,

m = IDC or the time elapsing between the first proposal and the final solution,

n = the number of extraneous issues brought into the discussion, and

p = the age of the Prohibitive Procrastinator,

$$x = \frac{(L + n)^m}{3p}$$

Then x is the amount of delay which is equal to denial.

*   *   *

At this point it is necessary to emphasise that the PP seldom says outright 'This cannot be done in your lifetime!' He allows this fact to emerge stealthily in the course of discussion.

'Our best method,' he will begin with apparent helpfulness, 'is to form a Committee on Procedure. This will produce an outline proposal, the various parts of which will be referred to sub-committees formed to deal with the legal, financial, cynical, technical, political, hysterical, statistical, ineffectual, and habitual aspects of the scheme. The sub-committees will report back to the Committee on Procedure, which will then issue an Interim Report. This should be laid before a Commission of Inquiry which will assemble not later than 1985. It will be the object of the Commission to recommend the procedures which we should adopt in deciding, first of all, whether there is a case for proceeding further in the matter.'

Pausing for breath, the PP will complete, on the back of an envelope, his calculation as to how much delay will equal negation. Having outlined a process which will continue until, say, 1987, he realises that 1990 is the target date. So he continues as follows:

'Supposing—and I emphasise that the question is more— much more—than a formality—*supposing* that there is a case for action, the Commission's final report will go to an inter-departmental Working Party, which will advise on the composition of the Planning Committee. It will be the task of the Planning Committee to approach the Permanent Under-Secretary of State, who will bring the matter before the Minister. Should his reaction be favourable, the matter will be brought up at the Party Conference at Skegness. It will be for the Party to decide whether the time is opportune, so soon before (or possibly so soon *after*) the General Election. In the light of that decision it will be for the Minister to issue a directive. He would not, however, at that stage, do more than accept the need, in principle, for further investigation.'

That is usually enough to end the matter without a single argument being used against the proposal under discussion. All the Reformer can see before him is an endless vista of committees trying to decide whether there is a case for making a preliminary inquiry into the terms of reference for a Commission. Comitology (the science of committee-sitting) is an old method of playing for time, but the techniques of delay have been strengthened in the modern world by the current emphasis on research. In matters scientific, the first rule, as we know, is to discover the facts. The same rule, as applied to human problems, means that a crime wave is not a matter of principle but of measurement. If Blacks riot in Los Angeles our first reaction is to count the Blacks, our second to decide whether they are as black as they are painted. That fact-finding is thus a substitute for decision is very generally known. What we fail to recognise is that fact-finding is also a substitute for thought. The months we spend on hearing the views of statisticians, psychologists, graphologists, sociologists, alchemists, and alienists are not merely months of inaction. Their effect is to smother our thought (as well as our action) in waves of irrelevance. We shall have to realise some day that reforms depend upon the existence of reformers with a general as well as a specialised knowledge, upon people who are often a law unto themselves, upon people who say 'Why not?' more often than 'Why?' and refuse to listen to the PP's covert opposition.

Army officers used to be taught, and indeed may still be

taught, how to make an Appreciation. In doing this, one used to begin (it might be) with a theoretical position of crisis. The enemy would be advancing from A towards B, the bridge being blown up at X and the railhead destroyed at Y, with all communication interrupted between you and the next higher formation. With shells bursting on all sides, the harassed officer was supposed to sit down and write 'Appreciation' at the top of a sheet of foolscap, underlining it before going on to add the details of his Aim, the Factors which might affect its Attainment, the Courses open to either side, and the Conclusion to which he was inescapably driven. No marks were ever awarded for concluding that the Army was the wrong profession to have chosen in the first place.

There can be no doubt, however, of the value of this mental exercise. Whether or not people actually do all this in battle, the logic of the Appreciation has much to commend it. And one would suppose that the commonest mistake of inexperience would be in a misinterpretation of the facts. In fact, however, the real stumbling block is always the *Aim* paragraph. For most people it is far more difficult to decide what they are trying to do than to describe how they propose to set about it. As for the factors which affect the situation, as seen from either side, they are only relevant in so far as they relate to the aim. If the aim is wrong, nothing else in the appreciation will be right. This observation is as true in peace as in war and the born Reformer is one who considers his aim first and the statistical position afterwards.

With his aim clearly in mind what is his next step? Surely, a memorandum. But here lies one of the most dangerous traps in his path. In former times, and even, it is rumoured, today, he would seek to give his ideas the widest circulation and have them printed or duplicated in large numbers. Because it was uneconomic in time and expense to set up the type or cut the stencil more than once, he always ordered spare copies. Where 78 people were to have copies he would order 100, just in case more would be needed; where 780, he would order 1,000. But the spare copies represented a waste, deplorable to any administrator. The natural reaction was to distribute them to those marginally interested in the issue. But each time even more copies were added, for distribution lists like many things have an innate principle of growth. And, just as inevitably, the lengthening list extended to people who were decreasingly literate. More and more people at lower and lower levels were spending longer and longer time reading what concerned them less and less.

It is here that the Reformer who wishes to outwit the PP finds to hand an unexpected ally in the form of a piece of modern technology. By dialling from a suitable machine a precise number of copies of a clearly thought-out and convincing memorandum—the number calculated on the basis of the effective decision-makers in his way—the Reformer bypasses both delay and unintelligence at one stroke. He gets his views in front of the right people at the right time.

Memoranda come from those who have done their thinking beforehand. In three respects the writer of a crisp memorandum with a specific circulation has an advantage over the PP. He has defined his purpose. He has undermined the confidence, in committee, of those who have failed to read it. And he has provided, quite probably, the basis of what will be agreed.

Parkinson's Law of Delay cannot, of course, be amended

or repealed but it can be circumvented. Just as it was within the bounds of ingenuity to accomplish human flight so, perhaps, there will always be a right way of getting new ideas off the ground.

12

Will of the People
or Annual General Meeting

WE ARE ALL FAMILIAR WITH THE BASIC DIFFERENCE
between British and French parliamentary institutions; copied respectively by such other assemblies as derive from
each. We all realise that this main difference has nothing
to do with national temperament, but stems from their
seating plans. The British, being brought up on team
games, enter their House of Commons in the spirit of those
who would rather be doing something else. If they cannot
be playing golf or tennis, they can at least pretend that
politics is a game with very similar rules. But for this
device, Parliament would arouse even less interest than it
does. So the British instinct is to form two opposing
teams, with referee and linesmen, and let them debate until
they exhaust themselves. The House of Commons is so
arranged that the individual Member is practically compelled to take one side or the other before he knows what
the arguments are, or even (in some cases) before he

knows the subject of the dispute. His training from birth has been to play for his side, and this saves him from any undue mental effort. Sliding into a seat toward the end of a speech, he knows exactly how to take up the argument from the point it has reached. If the speaker is on his own side of the House, he will say 'Hear, hear!' If he is on the opposite side, he can safely say 'Shame!' or merely 'Oh!' At some later stage he may have time to ask his neighbour what the debate is supposed to be about. Strictly speaking, however, there is no need for him to do this. He knows enough in any case not to kick into his own goal. The men who sit opposite are entirely wrong and all their arguments are so much drivel. The men on his own side are statesmanlike, by contrast, and their speeches a singular blend of wisdom, eloquence, and moderation. Nor does it make the slightest difference whether he learned his politics at Harrow or in following the fortunes of Aston Villa. In either school he will have learned when to cheer and when to groan. But the British system depends entirely on its seating plan. If the benches did not face each other, no one could tell truth from falsehood, wisdom from folly—unless indeed by listening to it all. But to listen to it all would be ridiculous, for half the speeches must of necessity be nonsense.

In France the initial mistake was made of seating the representatives in a semi-circle, all facing the chair. The resulting confusion could be imagined if it were not notorious. No real opposing teams could be formed and no one could tell (without listening) which argument was the more cogent. There was the further handicap of all the proceedings being in French—an example the United States wisely refused to follow. But the French system is bad enough even when the linguistic difficulty does not arise. Instead of having two sides, one in the right and the other in the wrong—so that the issue is clear from the outset—the French form a multitude of teams facing in all directions. With the field in such confusion, the game cannot even begin. Basically their representatives are of the Right or of the Left, according to where they sit. This is a perfectly sound scheme. The French have not gone to the extreme of seating people in alphabetical order. But the semi-circular chamber allows subtle distinctions between the various degrees of rightness and leftness. There is none of the clear-cut British distinction between rightness and wrongness. One deputy is described, politically, as to the left of Monsieur Untel but well to the right of Monsieur Quelquechose. What is anyone to make of that? What should we make of it even in English? What do they make of it themselves? The answer is, 'Nothing.'

All this is generally known. What is less generally recognised is that the paramount importance of the seating plan applies to other assemblies and meetings, international, national, and local. It applies, moreover, to meetings round a table such as occur at a Round Table Conference. A moment's thought will convince us that a Square Table Conference would be something totally different and a Long Table Conference would be different again. These differences do not merely affect the length and acrimony of the discussion; they also affect what (if anything) is decided. Rarely, as we know, will the voting relate to the merits of the case. The final decision is influenced by a variety of factors, few of which need concern us at the moment. We should note, however, that the issue is actually *decided,* in the end, by the votes of the centre bloc. This would not be true in the House of Commons, where no such bloc is allowed to develop. But at other conferences the centre bloc is all important. This bloc essentially comprises the following elements:

a. Those who have failed to master any one of the memoranda written in advance and showered weeks beforehand on all those who are expected to be present.

b. Those who are too stupid to follow the proceedings at all. These are readily distinguishable by their tendency to mutter to each other: 'What is the fellow talking about?'

c. Those who are deaf. They sit with their hands cupping their ears, growling, 'I wish people would speak up.'

d. Those who were dead drunk in the small hours and have turned up (heaven knows why) with a splitting headache and a conviction that nothing matters either way.

e. The senile, whose chief pride is in being as fit as ever—fitter indeed than a lot of these younger men. 'I *walked* here,' they whisper. 'Pretty good for a man of eighty-two, what?'

f. The feeble, who have weakly promised to support both sides and don't know what to do about it. They are of two minds as to whether they should abstain from voting or pretend to be sick.

Towards capturing the votes of the centre bloc the first step is to identify and count the members. That done, everything else depends on where they are to sit. The best technique is to detail off known and stalwart supporters to enter into conversation with named centre-bloc types before the meeting actually begins. In this preliminary chat the stalwarts will carefully avoid mentioning the main subject of debate. They will be trained to use the opening gambits listed below, corresponding to the categories listed above, into which the centre bloc naturally falls:

a. 'Waste of time, I call it, producing all these documents. I have thrown most of mine away.'

TACTICS

b. 'I expect we shall be dazzled by eloquence before long. I often wish people would talk less and come to the point. They are too clever by half, if you ask me.'

c. 'The acoustics of this hall are simply terrible. You would have thought these scientific chaps could do something about it. For half the time I CAN'T HEAR WHAT IS BEING SAID. CAN YOU?'

d. 'What a rotten place to meet! I think there is something the matter with the ventilation. It makes me feel almost unwell. What about you?'

e. 'My goodness, I don't know how you do it! Tell me the secret. Is it what you have for breakfast?'

f. 'There's so much to be said on both sides of the question that I really don't know which side to support. What do you feel about it?'

161

If these gambits are correctly played, each stalwart will start a lively conversation, in the midst of which he will steer his centre-blocsman toward the forum. As he does this, another stalwart will place himself just *ahead* of the pair and moving in the same direction. The drill is best illustrated by a concrete example. We will suppose that stalwart X (Mr Sturdy) is steering centre-blocsman Y (Mr Waverley, type *f*) toward a seat *near the front*. Ahead goes stalwart Z (Mr Staunch), who presently takes a seat without appearing to notice the two men following him. Staunch turns in the opposite direction and waves to someone in the distance. Then he leans over to make a few remarks to the man in front of him. Only when Waverley has sat down will Staunch presently turn toward him and say, 'My dear fellow—how nice to see you!' Only some minutes later again will he catch sight of Sturdy and start visibly with surprise. 'Hello, Sturdy—I didn't think you would be here!' 'I've recovered now,' replies Sturdy. 'It was only a chill.' The seating order is thus made to appear completely accidental, casual, and friendly. That completes Phase I of the operation, and it would be much the same whatever the exact category in which the centre-blocsman is believed to fall.

Phase II has to be adjusted according to the character of the man to be influenced. In the case of Waverley (type *f*) the object in Phase II is to avoid any discussion of the matter at issue but to produce the impression that the thing is already decided. Seated near the front, Waverley will be unable to see much of the other members and can be given the impression that they practically all think alike.

'Really,' says Sturdy, 'I don't know why I bothered to come. I gather that Item Four is pretty well agreed. All the fellows I meet seem to have made up their minds to vote for it.' (Or against it, as the case may be.)

'Curious,' says Staunch. 'I was just going to say the same thing. The issue hardly seems to be in doubt.'

'I had not really made up my own mind,' says Sturdy. 'There was much to be said on either side. But opposition would really be a waste of time. What do you think, Waverley?'

'Well,' says Waverley, 'I must admit that I find the question rather baffling. On the one hand, there is good reason to agree to the motion. . . . As against that. . . Do you think it will pass?'

'My dear Waverley, I would trust your judgement in this. You were saying just now that it is already agreed.'

'Oh, was I? Well, there does seem to be a majority. . . . Or perhaps I should say . . .'

'Thank you, Waverley,' says Staunch, 'for your opinion. I think just the same but am particularly interested to find you agree with me. There is no one whose opinion I value more.'

Sturdy, meanwhile, is leaning over to talk to someone in the row behind. What he actually says, in a low voice, is this: 'How is your wife now? Is she out of hospital?' When he turns back again, however, it is to announce that the people behind all think the same. The motion is as good as passed. And so it is if the drill goes according to plan.

While the other side has been busy preparing speeches and phrasing amendments, the side with the superior technique will have concentrated on pinning each centre-blocsman between two reliable supporters. When the crucial moment comes, the raising of a hand on either side will practically compel the waverer to follow suit. Should he be actually asleep, as often happens with centre-blocsmen in categories d and e, his hand will be raised for him by the member on his right. This rule is merely to obviate both his hands being raised, a gesture that has been known to attract unfavorable comment. With the centre bloc thus secured, the motion will be carried with a comfortable margin; or else rejected, if that is thought preferable. In nearly every matter of controversy to be decided by the will of the people, we can assume that the people who will decide are members of the centre bloc. Delivery of speeches is therefore a waste of time. The one party will never agree and the other party has agreed already. Remains the centre bloc, the members of which divide into those who cannot hear what is being said and those who would not understand it even if they did. To secure their votes what is needed is primarily the example of others voting on either side of them. Their votes can thus be swayed by accident. How much better, by contrast, to sway them by design!

STRUCTURE

13

Directors and Councils
or Coefficient of Inefficiency

THE LIFE CYCLE OF THE COMMITTEE IS SO BASIC TO OUR
knowledge of current affairs that it is surprising more
attention has not been paid to the science of comitology.
The first and most elementary principle of this science is
that a committee is organic rather than mechanical in its
nature: it is not a structure but a plant. It takes root and
grows, it flowers, wilts, and dies, scattering the seed from
which other committees will bloom in their turn. Only
those who bear this principle in mind can make real head-
way in understanding the structure and history of modern
government.

Committees, it is nowadays accepted, fall broadly into
two categories, those (a) from which the individual member has something to gain; and those (b) to which the
individual member merely has something to contribute.
Examples of the (b) group, however, are relatively unim-
portant for our purpose; indeed, some people doubt whether

they are committees at all. It is from the more robust (a)
group that we can learn most readily the principles which
are common (with modifications) to all. Of the (a) group
the most deeply rooted and luxuriant committees are those
which confer the most power and prestige upon their members. In most parts of the world these committees are
called 'cabinets.' This chapter is based on an extensive
study of national cabinets, over space and time.

When first examined under the microscope, the ideal
size of a cabinet council usually appears—to comitologists,
historians, and even to the people who appoint cabinets—
to be five. With that number the plant is viable, allowing
for two members to be absent or sick at any one time. Five
members are easy to collect and, when collected, can act
with competence, secrecy, and speed. Of these original
members four may well be versed, respectively, in finance, foreign policy, defence, and law. The fifth, who has
failed to master any of these subjects, usually becomes the
chairman or prime minister.

Whatever the apparent convenience might be of restricting the membership to five, however, we discover by
observation that the total number soon rises to seven or
nine. The usual excuse given for this increase, which is
almost invariable (exceptions being found, at one time, in
Luxembourg and Honduras) is the need for special knowledge on more than four topics. In fact, however, there is
another and more potent reason for adding to the team. For
in a cabinet of nine it will be found that policy is made by
three, information supplied by two, and financial warning
uttered by one. With the neutral chairman, that accounts
for seven, the other two appearing at first glance to be
merely ornamental. This allocation of duties was first noted
in England in about 1639, but there can be no doubt that
the folly of including more than three able and talkative

men in one committee had been discovered long before that. We know little as yet about the function of the two silent members but we have good reason to believe that a cabinet, in this second stage of development, might be unworkable without them.

There are cabinets in the world (those of Costa Rica, Ecuador, Northern Ireland, Liberia, the Philippines, Uruguay, and Panama will at once be called to mind) which long remained in this second stage—that is, by restricting their membership to nine. These remain, however, a small minority. Elsewhere and in larger territories cabinets have generally been subject to a law of growth. Other members come to be admitted, some with a claim to special knowledge but more because of their nuisance value when excluded. Their opposition can be silenced only by implicating them in every decision that is made. As they are brought in (and placated) one after another, the total membership rises from ten toward twenty. In this third stage of cabinets, there are already considerable drawbacks.

The most immediately obvious of these disadvantages is the difficulty of assembling people at the same place, date, and time. One member is going away on the 18th, whereas another does not return until the 21st. A third is never free on Tuesdays, and a fourth never available before 5 p.m. But that is only the beginning of the trouble, for, once most of them are collected, there is a far greater chance of members proving to be elderly, tiresome, inaudible, and deaf. Relatively few were chosen from any idea that they are or could be or have ever been useful. A majority perhaps were brought in merely to conciliate some outside group. Their tendency is therefore to report what happens to the group they represent. All secrecy is lost and, worst of all, members begin to prepare their speeches. They address the meeting and tell their friends afterwards about what they imagine they have said. But the more these merely representative members assert themselves, the more loudly do other outside groups clamour for representation. Internal parties form and seek to gain strength by further recruitment. The total of twenty is reached and passed. And thereby, quite suddenly, the cabinet enters the fourth and final stage of its history.

For at this point of cabinet development (between 20 and 22 members) the whole committee suffers an abrupt chemical or organic change. The nature of this change is easy to trace and comprehend. In the first place, the five members who matter will have taken to meeting before-hand. With decisions already reached, little remains for the nominal executive to do. And, as a consequence of this, all resistance to the committee's expansion comes to an end. More members will not waste more time; for the whole meeting is, in any case, a waste of time. So the pressure of outside groups is temporarily satisfied by the admission of their representatives, and decades may elapse before they realise how illusory their gain has been. With the doors wide open, membership rises from 20 to 30, from 30 to 40. There may soon be an instance of such a membership reaching the thousand mark. But this does not matter. For the cabinet has already ceased to be a real cabinet, and has been succeeded in its old functions by some other body.

Five times in English history has the plant moved through its life cycle. It would admittedly be difficult to prove that the first incarnation of the cabinet—the English Council of the Crown, now called the House of Lords—ever had a membership as small as five. When we first hear of it, indeed, its more intimate character has already been lost, with a hereditary membership varying from 29 to 50. Its subsequent expansion, however, kept pace with its loss of power. In round figures, it had 60 members in 1601, 140 in 1661, 220 in 1760, 400 in 1850, 650 in 1911, and 850 in 1952.

At what point in this progression did the inner committee appear in the womb of the peerage? It appeared in about 1257, its members being called the Lord of the King's Council and numbering less than 10. They numbered no more than 11 in 1378, and as few still in 1410. Then, from the reign of Henry V, they began to multiply. The 20 of 1433 had become the 41 of 1504, the total reaching 172 before the council finally ceased to meet.

Within the King's Council there developed the cabinet's third incarnation—the Privy Council—with an original membership of nine. It rose to 20 in 1540, to 29 in 1547, and to 44 in 1558. The Privy Council as it ceased to be effective increased proportionately in size. It had 47 members in 1679, 67 in 1723, 200 in 1902, and 300 in 1951.

Within the Privy Council there developed the junto or Cabinet Council, which effectively superseded the former in about 1615. Numbering 8 when we first hear of it, its members had come to number 12 by about 1700, and 20 by 1725. The Cabinet Council was then superseded in about 1740 by an inner group, since called simply the Cabinet.

From 1939, it will be apparent, there has been a struggle to save this institution; a struggle similar to the attempts made to save the Privy Council during the reign of Queen Elizabeth I. The Cabinet appeared to be in its decline in 1940, with an inner cabinet (of 5, 7, or 9 members) ready to take its place. More recent developments are best shown in tabular form:

Table I

THE BRITISH CABINET

Year	1740	1784	1801	1841	1885	1900	1915
No. of members	5	7	12	14	16	20	22

Year	1935	1939	1945	1945	1949	1954	1978
No. of members	22	23	16	20	17	18	24

Compared with the cabinet of Britain, the cabinet of the United States has shown an extraordinary resistance to political inflation. It had the appropriate number of 5 members in 1789, still only 7 by 1840, 9 by 1901, 10 by 1913, 11 by 1945, and 12 by 1978. In the meanwhile, the United States enjoys (with Guatemala and El Salvador) a reputation for cabinet-exclusiveness, having once had actually fewer cabinet ministers than Nicaragua or Paraguay.

STRUCTURE

Table II
SIZE OF CABINETS (1978)

No. of members	Countries
7	Switzerland
8	Iceland
9	Liberia, Uruguay
11	Luxembourg, Paraguay
12	United States
13	Colombia, Japan
14	Costa Rica, El Salvador
15	E. Germany, Finland, Norway
16	Brazil, Bulgaria, Eire, W. Germany, Netherlands, Peru
17	Dominican R., Yugoslavia
18	Austria, Burma, South Africa
19	Denmark, Israel, New Zealand, Spain
20	Bolivia, France, India, Sweden
21	Italy
22	Greece, Mexico
23	Belgium, Iran
24	Czechoslovakia, Egypt, Great Britain
26	Romania
28	Australia
33	Canada
35	Turkey
37	USSR
44	China

Note: The above figures are believed to have been correct at the time of going to press but readers must not assume that they are unalterable. Changes of administration bring about changes of organisation. The Table affords no more than a general basis of comparison.

How do other countries compare in this respect? The majority of non-totalitarian countries have cabinets that number between 12 and 20 members. Taking the average of over 60 countries, we find that it came at one time to over 16; the most popular numbers being 15 (seven instances) and 9 (seven again). Easily the oddest cabinet is that of New Zealand, one member of which had to be announced as 'Minister of Lands, Minister of Forests, Minister of Maori Affairs, Minister in charge of Maori Trust Office and of Scenery Preservation.' The toastmaster at a New Zealand banquet had equally to be ready to crave silence for 'The Minister of Health, Minister Assistant to the Prime Minister, Minister in Charge of State Advances Corporation, Census, and Statistics Department, Public Trust Office, and Publicity and Information.' In other lands this oriental profusion is fortunately rare.

A study of the British example would suggest that the point of ineffectiveness in a cabinet is reached when the total membership exceeds 20 or perhaps 21. The Council of the Crown, the King's Council, the Privy Council had each passed the 20 mark when their decline began. The British cabinet recoiled from the abyss before 1949 but has since tottered over the edge. We might be tempted to conclude from this that cabinets—or other committees—with a membership in excess of 21 are losing the reality of power and that those with a larger membership have already lost it. No such theory can be tenable, however, without statistical proof. Table II on the previous page attempts to furnish part of it.

Should we be justified in drawing a line in that table under the name of France (20 cabinet members) with an explanatory note to say that the cabinet is not the real power in countries shown below that line? Some comitologists would accept that conclusion without further research.

Others emphasise the need for careful investigation, more especially around the borderline of 21. But that the coefficient of inefficiency must lie between 19 and 22 is now very generally agreed.

What tentative explanation can we offer for this hypothesis? Here we must distinguish sharply between fact and theory, between the symptom and the disease. About the most obvious symptom there is little disagreement. It is known that with over 20 members present a meeting begins to change character. Conversations develop separately at either end of the table. To make himself heard, the member has therefore to rise. Once on his feet, he cannot help making a speech, if only from force of habit. 'Mr Chairman,' he will begin, 'I think I may assert without fear of contradiction—and I am speaking now from twenty-five (I might almost say twenty-seven) years of experience—that we must view this matter in the gravest light. A heavy responsibility rests upon us, sir, and I for one . . .'

Amid all this drivel the useful men present, if there are any, exchange little notes that read, 'Lunch with me tomorrow—we'll fix it then.'

What else can they do? The voice drones on interminably. The orator might just as well be talking in his sleep. The committee of which he is the most useless member has ceased to matter. It is finished. It is hopeless. It is dead.

So much is certain. But the root cause of the trouble goes deeper and has still, in part, to be explored. Too many vital factors are unknown. What is the shape and size of the table? What is the average age of those present? At what hour does the committee meet? In an article for the non-specialist it would be absurd to repeat the calculations by which the first and tentative coefficient of inefficiency has been reached. It should be enough to state that prolonged research at the Institute of Comitology has given rise to a formula which is now widely (although not universally) accepted by the experts in this field. It should perhaps be explained that the investigators assumed a temperate climate, leather-padded chairs, and a high level of sobriety. On this basis, the formula is as follows:

$$x = \frac{m^0 (a-d)}{y + p\sqrt{b}}$$

Where m = the average number of members actually present; ^{0} = the number of members influenced by outside pressure groups; a = the average age of the members; d = the distance in centimetres between the two members who are seated farthest from each other; y = the number of years since the cabinet or committee was first formed; p = the patience of the chairman, as measured on the Peabody scale; b = the average blood pressure of the three oldest members, taken shortly before the time of meeting. Then x = the number of members effectively present at the moment when the efficient working of the cabinet or other committee has become manifestly impossible. This is the coefficient of inefficiency and it is found to lie between 19.9 and 22.4. (The decimals represent partial attendance; those absent for a part of the meeting.)

It would be unsound to conclude, from a cursory inspection of this equation, that the science of comitology is in an advanced state of development. Comitologists and subcomitologists would make no such claim, if only from fear of unemployment. They emphasise, rather, that their studies have barely begun and that they are on the brink of astounding progress. Making every allowance for self-interest—which means discounting 90 per cent of what they say—we can safely assume that much work remains to be done.

We should eventually be able, for example, to learn the formula by which the optimum number of committee members may be determined. Somewhere between the number of three (when a quorum is impossible to collect) and approximately 21 (when the whole organism begins to perish), there lies the golden number. The interesting theory has been propounded that this number must be eight. Why? Because it is the only number which all existing states with the exception of Iceland (see Table II) have agreed to avoid. Attractive as this theory may seem at first sight, it is open to one serious objection. Eight was the number preferred by King Charles I for his Committee of State. And look what happened to him!

14

Injelititis
or Palsied Paralysis

WE FIND EVERYWHERE A TYPE OF ORGANISATION (AD-ministrative, commercial, or academic) in which the higher officials are plodding and dull, those less senior are active only in intrigue against each other, and the junior men are frustrated or frivolous. Little is being attempted. Nothing is being achieved. And in contemplating this sorry picture, we conclude that those in control have done their best, struggled against adversity, and have finally admitted defeat. It now appears from the results of recent investigation, that no such failure need be assumed. In a high percentage of the moribund institutions so far examined the final state of coma is something gained of set purpose and after prolonged effort. It is the result, admittedly, of a disease, but of a disease that is largely self-induced. From the first signs of the condition, the progress of the disease has been encouraged, the cause aggravated, and the symptoms welcomed. It is the disease of induced inferiority, called Injelititis. It is a commoner ailment than is often supposed, and the diagnosis is far easier than the cure.

Our study of the organisational paralysis begins, logically, with a description of the course of the disease from the first signs to the final coma. The second stage of our inquiry concerns symptoms and diagnosis. The third stage should properly include some reference to treatment, but little is known about this. Nor is much likely to be discovered in the immediate future, for the tradition of British medical research is entirely opposed to any emphasis on this part of the subject. British medical specialists are usually quite content to trace the symptoms and define the cause. It is the French, by contrast, who begin by describing the treatment and discuss the diagnosis later, if at all. We feel bound to adhere in this to the British method, which may not help the patient but which is unquestionably more scientific. To travel hopefully is better than to arrive.

The first sign of danger is represented by the appearance in the organisation's hierarchy of an individual who combines in himself a high concentration of incompetence and jealousy. Neither quality is significant in itself and most people have a certain proportion of each. But when these two qualities reach a certain concentration—represented at present by the formula I_3J_5—there is a chemical reaction. The two elements fuse, producing a new substance that we have termed 'injelitance.' The presence of this substance can be safely inferred from the actions of any individual who, having failed to make anything of his own department, tries constantly to interfere with other departments and gain control of the central administration. The specialist who observes this particular mixture of failure and ambition will at once shake his head and murmur, 'Primary or idiopathic injelitance.' The symptoms, as we shall see, are quite unmistakable.

STRUCTURE

The next or secondary stage in the progress of the disease is reached when the infected individual gains complete or partial control of the central organisation. In many instances this stage is reached without any period of primary infection, the individual having actually entered the organisation at that level. The injelitant individual is easily recognisable at this stage from the persistence with which he struggles to eject all those abler than himself, as also from his resistance to the appointment or promotion of anyone who might prove abler in course of time. He dare not say, 'Mr Asterisk is too able,' so he says, 'Asterisk? Clever, perhaps—but is he *sound*? I incline to prefer Mr Cypher.' He dare not say, 'Mr Asterisk makes me feel small,' so he says, 'Mr Cypher appears to me to have the better judgement.' Judgement is an interesting word that signifies in this context the opposite of intelligence; it means, in fact, doing what was done last time. So Mr Cypher is promoted and Mr Asterisk goes elsewhere. The central administration gradually fills up with people more stupid than the chairman, director, or manager. If the head of the organisation is second-rate, he will see to it that his immediate staff are all third-rate; and they will, in turn, see to it that their subordinates are fourth-rate. There will soon be an actual competition in stupidity, people pretending to be even more brainless than they are.

The next or tertiary stage in the onset of this disease is reached when there is no spark of intelligence left in the whole organisation from top to bottom. This is the state of coma we described in our first paragraph. When that stage has been reached the institution is, for all practical purposes, dead. It may remain in a coma for twenty years. It may quietly disintegrate. It may even, finally, recover. Cases of recovery are rare. It may be thought odd that recovery without treatment should be possible. The process is quite natural, nevertheless, and closely resembles the process by which various living organisms develop a resistance to poisons that are at first encounter fatal. It is as if the whole institution had been sprayed with a DDT solution guaranteed to eliminate all ability found in its way. For a period of years this practice achieves the desired result. Eventually, however, individuals develop an immunity. They conceal their ability under a mask of imbecile good humour. The result is that the operatives assigned to the task of ability-elimination fail (through stupidity) to recognise ability when they see it. An individual of merit penetrates the outer defences and begins to make his way toward the top. He wanders on, babbling about golf and giggling feebly, losing documents and forgetting names, and looking just like everyone else. Only when he has reached high rank does he suddenly throw off the mask and appear like the demon king among a crowd of panto-mime fairies. With shrill screams of dismay the high exec-utives find ability right there in the midst of them. It is too late by then to do anything about it. The damage has been done, the disease is in retreat, and full recovery is possible over the next ten years. But these instances of natural cure are extremely rare. In the more usual course of events, the disease passes through the recognised stages and becomes, as it would seem, incurable.

We have seen what the disease is. It now remains to show by which symptoms its presence can be detected. It is one thing to detail the spread of the infection in an imaginary case, classified from the start. It is quite a different thing to enter a factory, barracks, office, or col-lege and recognise the symptoms at a glance. We all know how an estate agent will wander round a vacant house when acting for the purchaser. It is only a question of time before he throws open a cupboard or kicks a skirting and exclaims, 'Dry rot!' (acting for the vendor, he would lose the key of the cupboard while drawing attention to the view from the window). In the same way a political scientist can recognise the symptoms of Injelititis even in its primary stage. He will pause, sniff, and nod wisely, and it should be obvious at once that he *knows*. But how does he know? How can he tell that injelitance has set in? If the original source of the infection were present, the diagnosis would be easier, but it is still quite possible when the germ of the disease is on holiday. His influence can be detected in the atmosphere. It can be detected, above all, in certain remarks that will be made by others, as thus: 'It would be a mistake for us to attempt too much. We cannot compete with Toprank. Here in Lowgrade we do useful work, meeting the needs of the country. Let us be content with that.' Or again, 'We do not pretend to be in the first flight. It is absurd the way these people at Much-Striving talk of their work, just as if they were in the Toprank class.' Or finally, 'Some of our younger men have transferred to Toprank—one or two even to Much-Striving. It is probably their wisest plan. We are quite happy to let them succeed in that way. An exchange of ideas and personnel is a good thing—although, to be sure, the few men we have had from Toprank have been rather disappointing. We can only expect the people they have thrown out. Ah, well, we must not grumble. We always avoid friction when we can. And, in our humble way, we can claim to be doing a good job.'

What do these remarks suggest? They suggest—or rather, they clearly indicate—that the standard of achievement has been set too low. Only a low standard is desired and one still lower is acceptable. The directives issuing from a second-rate chief and addressed to his third-rate executives speak only of minimum aims and ineffectual means. A higher standard of competence is not desired, for an efficient organisation would be beyond the chief's power to control. The motto, 'Ever third-rate' has been inscribed over the main entrance in letters of gold. Third-rateness has become a principle of policy. It will be observed, however, that the existence of higher standards is still recognised. There remains at this stage a hint of apology, a feeling of uneasiness when Toprank is mentioned. Neither this apology nor unease lasts for long. The second stage of the disease comes on quickly and it is this we must now describe.

The secondary stage is recognised by its chief symptom, which is smugness. The aims have been set low and have therefore been largely achieved. The target has been set up within ten yards of the firing point and the scoring has therefore been high. The directors have done what they set out to do. This soon fills them with self-satisfaction. They set out to do something and they have done it. They soon forget that it was a small effort to gain a small result. They observe only that they have succeeded—unlike those people at Much-Striving. They become increasingly smug and their smugness reveals itself in remarks such as this: 'The chief is a sound man and very clever when you get to know him. He never says much—that is not his way—but he seldom makes a mistake.' (These last words can be said with justice of someone who never does anything at all.) Or this: 'We rather distrust brilliance here. These clever people can be a dreadful nuisance, upsetting established routine and proposing all sorts of schemes that we have never seen tried. We obtain splendid results by simple common sense and teamwork.' And finally this: 'Our canteen is something we are really rather proud of. We don't know how the caterer can produce as good a lunch at the price. We are lucky to have him!' This last remark is made as we sit at a table covered with dirty oilcloth, facing an uneatable, nameless mess on a plate and shuddering at the sight and smell of what passes for coffee. In point of fact, the canteen reveals more than the office. Just as for a quick verdict we judge a private house by inspection of the WC (to find whether there is a spare toilet roll), just as we judge a hotel by the state of the cruet, so we judge a larger institution by the appearance of the canteen. If the decoration is in dark brown and pale green; if the curtains are purple (or absent); if there are no flowers in sight; if there is barley in the soup (with or without a dead fly); if the menu is one of hash and mould; and if the executives are still delighted with everything—why, then the institution is in a pretty bad way. For self-satisfaction, in such a case, has reached the point at which those responsible cannot tell the difference between food and filth. This is smugness made absolute.

The tertiary and last stage of the disease is one in which apathy has taken the place of smugness. The executives no longer boast of their efficiency as compared with some other institution. They have forgotten that any other institution exists. They have ceased to eat in the canteen, preferring now to bring sandwiches and scatter their desks with the crumbs. The notice boards carry notices about the concert that took place four years ago. Mr. Brown's office has a nameplate saying, 'Mr Smith.' Mr Smith's door is marked, 'Mr Robinson,' in faded ink on an adhesive luggage label. The broken windows have been repaired with odd bits of cardboard. The electric light switches give a slight but painful shock when touched. The whitewash is flaking off the ceiling and the paint is blotchy on the walls. The lift is out of order and the cloakroom tap cannot be turned off. Water from the broken skylight drips wide of the bucket placed to catch it, and from somewhere in the basement comes the wail of a hungry cat. The last stage of the disease has brought the whole organisation to the point of collapse. The symptoms of the disease in this acute form are so numerous and evident that a trained investigator can often detect them over the telephone without visiting the place at all. When a weary voice answers ''Ullo!' (that most unhelpful of replies), the expert has often heard enough. He shakes his head sadly as he replaces the receiver. 'Well on in the tertiary phase,' he will mutter to himself, 'and almost certainly inoperable.' It is too late to attempt any sort of treatment. The institution is practically dead.

We have now described this disease as seen from within and then again from outside. We know now the origin, the progress, and the outcome of the infection, as also the symptoms by which its presence is detected. British medical skill seldom goes beyond that point in its research.

STRUCTURE

Once a disease has been identified, named, described, and accounted for, the British are usually quite satisfied and ready to investigate the next problem that presents itself. If asked about treatment they look surprised and suggest the use of penicillin preceded or followed by the extraction of all the patient's teeth. It becomes clear at once that this is not an aspect of the subject that interests them. Should our attitude be the same? Or should we as political scientists consider what, if anything, can be done about it? It would be premature, no doubt, to discuss any possible treatment in detail, but it might be useful to indicate very generally the lines along which a solution might be attempted. Certain principles, at least, might be laid down. Of such principles, the first would have to be this: a diseased institution cannot reform itself. There are instances, we know, of a disease vanishing without treatment, just as it appeared without warning; but these cases are rare and regarded by the specialist as irregular and undesirable. The cure, whatever its nature, must come from outside. For a patient to remove his own appendix under a local anaesthetic may be physically possible, but the practice is regarded with disfavour and is open to many objections. Other operations lend themselves still less to the patient's own dexterity. The first principle we can safely enunciate is that the patient and the surgeon should not be the same person. When an institution is in an advanced state of disease, the services of a specialist are required and even, in some instances, the services of the greatest living authority: Parkinson himself. The fees payable may be very heavy indeed, but in a case of this sort, expense is clearly no object. It is a matter, after all, of life and death.

The second principle we might lay down is this, that the primary stage of the disease can be treated by a simple injection, that the secondary stage can be cured in some

187

instances by surgery, and that the tertiary stage must be regarded at present as incurable. There was a time when physicians used to babble about bottles and pills, but this is mainly out of date. There was another period when they talked more vaguely about psychology; but that too is out of date, most of the psychoanalysts having since been certified as insane. The present age is one of injections and incisions and it behoves the political scientists to keep in step with the Faculty. Confronted by a case of primary infection, we prepare a syringe automatically and only hesitate as to what, besides water, it should contain. In principle, the injection should contain some active substance—but from which group should it be selected? A kill-or-cure injection would contain a high proportion of Intolerance, but this drug is difficult to procure and sometimes too powerful to use. Intolerance is obtainable from the bloodstream of regimental sergeant majors and is found to comprise two chemical elements, namely: (a) the best is scarcely good enough (GG^{nth}) and (b) there is no excuse for anything (NE^{nth}). Injected into a diseased institution, the intolerant individual has a tonic effect and may cause the organism to turn against the original source of infection. While this treatment may well do good, it is by no means certain that the cure will be permanent. It is doubtful, that is to say, whether the infected substance will be actually expelled from the system. Such information as we have rather leads us to suppose that this treatment is merely palliative in the first instance, the disease remaining latent though inactive. Some authorities believe that repeated injections would result in a complete cure, but others fear that repetition of the treatment would set up a fresh irritation, only slightly less dangerous than the original disease. Intolerance is a drug to be used, therefore, with caution.

There exists a rather milder drug called Ridicule, but its

operation is uncertain, its character unstable, and its effects too little known. There is little reason to fear that any damage could result from an injection of ridicule, but neither is it evident that a cure would result. It is generally agreed that the injelitant individual will have developed a thick protective skin, insensitive to ridicule. It may well be that ridicule may tend to isolate the infection, but that is as much as could be expected and more indeed than has been claimed.

We may note, finally, that Castigation, which is easily obtainable, has been tried in cases of this sort and not wholly without effect. Here again, however, there are difficulties. This drug is an immediate stimulus but can produce a result the exact opposite of what the specialist intends. After a momentary spasm of activity, the injelitant individual will often prove more supine than before and just as harmful as a source of infection. If any use can be made of castigation it will almost certainly be as one element in a preparation composed otherwise of intolerance and ridicule, with perhaps other drugs as yet untried. It only remains to point out that this preparation does not as yet exist.

The secondary stage of the disease we believe to be operable. Professional readers will all have heard of the Nuciform Sack and of the work generally associated with the name of Cutler Walpole. The operation first performed by that great surgeon involves, simply, the removal of the infected parts and the simultaneous introduction of new blood drawn from a similar organism. This operation has sometimes succeeded. It is only fair to add that it has also sometimes failed. The shock to the system can be too great. The new blood may be unobtainable and may fail, even when procured, to mingle with the blood previously in circulation. On the other hand, this drastic method offers, beyond question, the best chance of a complete cure.

The tertiary stage presents us with no opportunity to do anything. The institution is for all practical purposes dead. It can be founded afresh but only with a change of name, a change of site, and an entirely different staff. The temptation, for the economically minded, is to transfer some portion of the original staff to the new institution—in the name, for example, of continuity. Such a transfusion would certainly be fatal, and continuity is the very thing to avoid. No portion of the old and diseased foundation can be regarded as free from infection. No staff, no equipment, no tradition must be removed from the original site. Strict quarantine should be followed by complete disinfection. Infected personnel should be dispatched with a warm testimonial to such rival institutions as are regarded with particular hostility. All equipment and files should be destroyed without hesitation. As for the buildings, the best plan is to insure them heavily and then set them alight. Only when the site is a blackened ruin can we feel certain that the germs of the disease are dead.

15

Plans and Plants
or Administration Block

EVERY STUDENT OF HUMAN INSTITUTIONS IS FAMILIAR
with the standard test by which the importance of the
individual may be assessed. The number of doors to be
passed, the number of his personal assistants, the number
of his telephone receivers—these three figures, taken with
the depth of his carpet in centimetres, has given us a
simple formula that is reliable for most parts of the world.
It is less widely known that the same sort of measurement
is applicable, *but in reverse*, to the institution itself.

Take, for example, a publishing organisation. Publishers
have a strong tendency, as we know, to live in a state of
chaotic squalor. The visitor who applies at the obvious
entrance is led outside and around the block, down an
alley and up three flights of stairs. A research establishment is similarly housed, as a rule, on the ground floor of
what was once a private house, a crazy wooden corridor
leading thence to a corrugated-iron hut in what was once

the garden. Are we not all familiar, moreover, with the layout of an international airport? As we emerge from the aircraft, we see (over to our right or left) a lofty structure wrapped in scaffolding. Then the air hostess leads us into a hut with an asbestos roof. Nor do we suppose for a moment that it will ever be otherwise. By the time the building is complete the airfield will have been moved to another site.

The institutions already mentioned—lively and productive as they may be—flourish in such shabby and makeshift surroundings that we might turn with relief to an institution clothed from the outset with convenience and dignity. The outer door, in bronze and glass, is placed centrally in a symmetrical façade. Polished shoes glide quietly over shining rubber to the glittering and silent lift. The overpoweringly cultured receptionist will murmur with carmine lips into an ice-blue receiver. She will wave you into a chromium armchair, consoling you with a dazzling smile for any slight but inevitable delay. Looking up from a glossy magazine, you will observe how the wide corridors radiate toward departments A, B, and C. From behind closed doors will come the subdued noise of an ordered activity. A minute later and you are ankle deep in the director's carpet, plodding sturdily toward his distant, tidy desk. Hypnotised by the chief's unwavering stare, cowed by the Matisse hung upon his wall, you will feel that you have found real efficiency at last.

In point of fact you will have discovered nothing of the kind. It is now known that a perfection of planned layout is achieved only by institutions on the point of collapse. This apparently paradoxical conclusion is based upon a wealth of archaeological and historical research, with the more esoteric details of which we need not concern ourselves. In general principle, however, the method pursued has been to select and date the buildings which appear to have been perfectly designed for their purpose. A study and comparison of these has tended to prove that perfection of planning is a symptom of decay. During a period of exciting discovery or progress there is no time to plan the perfect headquarters. The time for that comes later, when all the important work has been done. Perfection, we know, is finality; and finality is death.

Thus, to the casual tourist, awestruck in front of St Peter's, Rome, the Basilica, and the Vatican must seem the ideal setting for the Papal Monarchy at the very height of its prestige and power. Here, he reflects, must Innocent III have thundered his anathema. Here must Gregory VII have laid down the law. But a glance at the guide-book will convince the traveller that the really powerful Popes reigned long before the present dome was raised, and reigned not infrequently somewhere else. More than that, the later Popes lost half their authority while the work was still in progress. Julius II, whose decision it was to build, and Leo X, who approved Raphael's design, were dead long before the buildings assumed their present shape. Bramante's palace was still being built until 1565, the great church not consecrated until 1626, nor the piazza colonnades finished until 1667. The great days of the Papacy were over before the perfect setting was even planned. They were almost forgotten by the date of its completion.

That this sequence of events is in no way exceptional can be proved with ease. Just such a sequence can be found in the history of the League of Nations. Great hopes centred on the League from its inception in 1920 until about 1930. By 1933, at the latest, the experiment was seen to have failed. Its physical embodiment, however, the Palace of the Nations, was not opened until 1937. It was a structure no doubt justly admired. Deep thought had gone into the design of secretariat and council chambers, committee rooms and cafeteria. Everything was there which ingenuity could devise—except, indeed, the League itself. By the year when its Palace was formally opened the League had practically ceased to exist.

It might be urged that the Palace of Versailles is an instance of something quite opposite; the architectural embodiment of Louis XIV's monarchy at its height. But here again the facts refuse to fit the theory. For granted that Versailles may typify the triumphant spirit of that age, it was mostly completed very late in the reign, and some of it indeed during the reign that followed. The building of Versailles mainly took place between 1669 and 1685. The king did not move there until 1682, and even then the work was still in progress. The famous royal bedroom was not occupied until 1701, nor the chapel finished until nine years later. Considered as a seat of government, rather than a royal residence, Versailles dates in part from as late as 1756. On the other hand, Louis XIV's real triumphs were mostly before 1679, the apex of his career being reached in 1682 itself and his power declining from about 1685. According to one historian, Louis, in coming to Versailles, 'was already sealing the doom of his line and race.' Another says of Versailles that 'The whole thing . . . was completed just when the decline of Louis' power had begun.' A third tacitly supports this theory by describing the period 1685–1713 as 'The Years of Decline.' In other words, the visitor who thinks Versailles the place from which Turenne rode forth to victory is essentially mistaken. It would be historically more correct to picture the embarrassment, in that setting, of those who came with the news of defeat at Blenheim. In a palace resplendent with emblems of victory they can hardly have known which way to look.

STRUCTURE

Mention of Blenheim must naturally call to mind the palace of that name built for the victorious Duke of Marlborough. Here again we have a building ideally planned, this time as the place of retirement for a national hero. Its heroic proportions are more dramatic perhaps than convenient, but the general effect is just what the architects intended. No scene could more fittingly enshrine a legend. No setting could have been more appropriate for the meeting of old comrades on the anniversary of a battle. Our pleasure, however, in picturing the scene is spoiled by our realisation that it cannot have taken place. The Duke never lived there and never even saw it finished. His actual residence was at Holywell, near St Albans and (when in town) at Marlborough House. He died at Windsor Lodge and his old comrades, when they held a reunion, are known to have dined in a tent. Blenheim took long in building, not because of the elaboration of the design—which was admittedly quite elaborate enough—but because the Duke was in disgrace and even, for two years, in exile during the period which might otherwise have witnessed its completion.

What of the monarchy which the Duke of Marlborough served? Just as tourists now wander, guide-book in hand, through the Orangerie or the Galerie des Glaces, so the future archaeologist may peer around what once was London. And he may well incline to see in the ruins of Buckingham Palace a true expression of British monarchy. He will trace the great avenue from Admiralty Arch to the palace gate. He will reconstruct the forecourt and the central balcony, thinking all the time how suitable it must have been for a powerful ruler whose sway extended to the remote parts of the world. Even a present-day American might be tempted to shake his head over the arrogance of a George III, enthroned in such impressive state as this. But

195

again we find that the really powerful monarchs all lived somewhere else, in buildings long since vanished—at Greenwich or Nonesuch, Kenilworth or Whitehall. The builder of Buckingham Palace was George IV, whose court architect, John Nash, was responsible for what was described at the time as its 'general feebleness and triviality of taste.' But George IV himself, who lived at Carlton House or Brighton, never saw the finished work; nor did William IV, who ordered its completion. It was Queen Victoria who first took up residence there in 1837, being married from the new palace in 1840. But her first enthusiasm for Buckingham Palace was relatively short-lived. Her husband infinitely preferred Windsor and her own later preference was for Balmoral or Osborne. The splendours of Buckingham Palace are therefore to be associated, if we are to be accurate, with a later and strictly constitutional monarchy. It dates from a period when power was vested in Parliament.

It is natural, therefore, to ask at this point whether the Palace of Westminster, where the House of Commons meets, is itself a true expression of parliamentary rule. It represents beyond question a magnificent piece of planning, aptly designed for debate and yet provided with ample space for everything else—for committee meetings, for quiet study, for refreshment, and (on its terrace) for tea. It has everything a legislator could possibly desire, all incorporated in a building of immense dignity and comfort. It should date—but this we now hardly dare assume—from a period when parliamentary rule was at its height. But once again the dates refuse to fit into this pattern. The original House, where Pitt and Fox were matched in oratory, was accidentally destroyed by fire in 1834. It would appear to have been as famed for its inconvenience as for its lofty standard of debate. The present structure was begun in 1840, partly occupied in 1852, but incomplete when its architect died in 1860. It finally assumed its present appearance in about 1868. Now, by what we can no longer regard as coincidence, the decline of Parliament can be traced, without much dispute, to the Reform Act of 1867. It was in the following year that all initiative in legislation passed from Parliament to be vested in the Cabinet. The prestige attached to the letters 'M.P.' began sharply to decline and thenceforward the most that could be said is that 'a role, though a humble one, was left for private members.' The great days were over.

The same could not be said of the various Ministries, which were to gain importance in proportion to Parliament's decline. Investigation may yet serve to reveal that the India Office reached its peak of efficiency when accommodated in the Westminster Palace Hotel. What is more significant, however, is the development of the former Colonial Office. For while the British Empire was mostly acquired at a period when the Colonial Office (in so far as there was one) occupied haphazard premises in Downing Street, a new phase of colonial policy began when the department moved into buildings actually designed for the purpose. This was in 1875 and the structure was well designed as a background for the disasters of the Boer War. But the Colonial Office gained a new lease of life during World War II. With its move to temporary and highly inconvenient premises in Great Smith Street—premises leased from the Church of England and intended for an entirely different purpose—British colonial policy entered that phase of enlightened activity which will end no doubt with the final collapse of the Commonwealth. No date for this has as yet been announced.

But no other British example can now match in significance the story of New Delhi. Nowhere else have British

architects been given the task of planning so great a capital
city as the seat of government for so vast a population.
The intention to found New Delhi was announced at the
Imperial Durbar of 1911, King George V being at that
time the Mogul's successor on what had been the Peacock
Throne. Sir Edwin Lutyens then proceeded to draw up
plans for a British Versailles, splendid in conception, comprehensive in detail, masterly in design, and overpowering
in scale. But the stages of its progress toward completion
correspond with so many steps in political collapse. The
Government of India Act of 1909 had been the prelude to
all that followed—the attempt on the Viceroy's life in
1912, the Declaration of 1917, the Montagu-Chelmsford
Report of 1918, and its implementation in 1920. Lord Irwin
actually moved into his new palace in 1929, the year in
which the Indian Congress demanded independence, the
year in which the Round Table Conference opened, the

year before the Civil Disobedience campaign began. It would be possible, though tedious, to trace the whole story down to the day when the British finally withdrew, showing how each phase of the retreat was exactly paralleled with the completion of another triumph in civic design. What was finally achieved was no more and no less than a mausoleum.

The decline of British imperialism actually began with the general election of 1906 and the victory on that occasion of liberal and semi-socialist ideas. It need surprise no one, therefore, to observe that 1906 is the date of completion carved in imperishable granite over the War Office doors. The campaign of Waterloo might have been directed from poky offices around the Horse Guards Parade. It was, by contrast, in surroundings of dignity that were approved the plans for attacking the Dardanelles. Might it be that the elaborate layout of the Pentagon at Arlington, Virginia, provides another significant lesson for planners? It would be unfair to detect an element of logic in the siting of the Pentagon alongside the National Cemetery, but the subject seems at least worthy of investigation.

It is by no means certain that an influential reader of this chapter could prolong the life of a dying institution merely by depriving it of its streamlined headquarters. What he can do, however, with more confidence, is to prevent any organisation strangling itself at birth. Examples abound of new institutions coming into existence with a full establishment of deputy directors, consultants, and executives, all these coming together in a building specially designed for their purpose. And experience proves that such an institution will die. It is choked by its own perfection. It cannot take root for lack of soil. It cannot grow naturally for it is already grown. Fruitless by its very nature, it cannot even flower. When we see an example of such planning—when we are confronted for example by the building designed for the United Nations—the experts among us shake their heads sadly, draw a sheet over the corpse, and tiptoe quietly into the open air.

THE LAW

16

Law of the Vacuum
or Hoover for President

PARKINSON'S FIRST LAW, WHICH GOVERNS THE RELA-
tionship between work and time has never been disproved,
whether by argument, experience, research, or thought. As
a corollary to the central theory is the obvious conclusion
that any administrative staff must increase in number by a
known percentage irrespective of the work (if any) to be
done. In public administration, moreover, there have been
instances of expansion far exceeding what seemed to be
the norm. Generally speaking the validity of the Law has
been proved by subsequent events but with certain exceptions which have to be admitted. For one thing, Parkinson's Law has itself had its impact, those who have studied
it finding the means to circumvent it, just as careful students of *Das Kapital* know how to frustrate the spread of
Marxism. There are instances, especially in private enterprise, of administrative proliferation being checked or even
reversed. A leading German corporation once reduced its

central office staff from 2,000 to 250. Something is being done to reduce the governmental burden in the State of California. Events such as these are not a matter of daily occurrence but they do happen from time to time.

These exceptions prove the rule but it could be argued that the Law, although generally accepted, deserves a better explanation than it has ever had. It has, in point of fact, been studied over the years and all the work done points to the conclusion that Parkinson's Law is one aspect of a more general Law:

ACTION EXPANDS TO FILL THE VOID
CREATED BY HUMAN FAILURE.

Take a specific example. A large industrial group in England came under the managing direction of an industrialist so eminent that he later achieved a peerage. Looking around the central plant he observed that the administrative offices were scattered over the whole complex, some accommodated in temporary wooden huts of a design fashionable during World War I, others in more recent structures which may or may not have been originally planned as bicycle sheds. He resolved to concentrate all these offices under one roof, not because this would make for greater efficiency (it doesn't, as he well knew) but because it would reduce the total sum payable in rates or municipal taxation. The new office building, revolting in its modernity, was completed and declared open with all the pomp which normally marks the completion of any building which is sufficiently hideous. Had the organisation been perfect the cutting of the tape at the main entrance should have coincided with the blast of a whistle, the signal for the bulldozers to demolish the old offices, the sites of which should have been levelled by sunset. Even as distinguished a man as the Managing Director had forgotten that office staff will always multiply so as to fill the office space available. On the opening day of the new administrative block all the new offices were occupied by office staff. A week later all the old offices, scheduled as they were for demolition, were as fully occupied and as busy as before. An apparently good idea had produced disastrous results, not so much because of the money wasted as because of the greater inefficiency which goes with greater numbers.

The same general principle applies to the drama of the

take-over bid. We have all heard of the wizards of finance who terrorise the City and make vast fortunes from the annexation, amalgamation, and reorganisation of businesses, actually ailing, which we had all regarded as monumental in their solidity. What firm is safe, we ask ourselves, while these pirates range the stock markets? Can no law be framed to protect the possible victims? But here again the basic fault lies in the awful complacency of portly directors who fail to realise how vulnerable their position has become. By leaving early and coming late these self-satisfied men prepare the way for their own downfall. They are unenterprising, inactive, ignorant, and old. But the business which is not imaginative and dynamic has already begun to decline and it is the vacuum created by its decay which attracts the takeover bid just as its internal inertia causes industrial dispute. The plant which ceases to blossom has begun, in fact, to die. All this may seem obvious enough but we seldom notice that the truth about the vulnerable firm applies also to free enterprise as a whole. We recognise the external pressures quickly enough. Communist countries present a military threat, preceded by the more insidious processes of infiltration. Communist or semi-communist internal parties present a different sort of threat, making use of industrial unrest and the rusting machinery of the democratic process. Aware of these dangers, businessmen react with belated indignation and protest. What they fail to see is that the fault lies at least partly within themselves.

A declining institution, whether a country, a university, a trade union, or a business enterprise, is one in which the leaders have lost their way, have forgotten above all what exactly they are trying to do. The creation of the vacuum is due to basic causes which need for their proper analysis not a page but a book. If the causes are obscure and complex, however, the symptoms are obvious and one of them is the failure to communicate. There are other symptoms, heaven knows, some to be found in the balance sheet, others in the sorry tale of government by deficit, but it is proper to emphasise what the most casual observer must notice first. We judge an industrial or commercial enterprise by the attractiveness or otherwise of the girl at the reception desk. We judge a university by the wealth and variety of books on sale at the campus bookstore or in the adjacent high street bookshops. We judge a military unit by the way the officers group themselves in mess. But we also judge every kind of institution by the message it has for the world. Every building, for example, has a message to convey; often no more than the statement 'We wanted ten per cent on the outlay.' But where a building will always say something, however sordid or banal, an organisation will often fail to say anything and this we describe as a failure to communicate.

Communication, upon which all civilisation depends, involves the transmission between people of emotions, facts, ideas, or instruction. To succeed in the art of communication we must have the wish to communicate, the ability to create trust, a clear idea of what we want to say, and, finally, a sense of style. We must realise that whereas most people want to talk few of them have anything to say. What organisation men say or write or print often means nothing at all, being merely the bureaucratic equivalent of breaking wind. To succeed in the art of communication we have to make a big effort and it is initially an effort of imagination. We have to put ourselves in the position of the people we seek to influence, which is for most of us the most difficult task of all.

At the Battle of Balaclava Lord Raglan sent a message to Lord Lucan, telling him to attack the enemy guns. From where he was, on a hill-top, it was perfectly clear what he meant. Down in a valley Lord Lucan had a different view of the battlefield which did not include the cannon which Lord Raglan wanted to recapture but did include whole batteries to which he had not meant to refer. On Lucan's orders Lord Cardigan charged them at the head of the Light Brigade, which was totally destroyed. The point to emphasize is that Lord Raglan, who had many virtues, lacked the imagination needed to realise what the battle-field looked like from a different angle, and indeed on a different level. This sort of mistake is repeated every day and is always the result of a failure to see the situation from someone else's point of view.

Given the desire to communicate and given some imagination, our next task is to ensure that people will believe what we say and accept what we promise. It is no good saying: 'Trust me. Rely on my word.' Only politicians say that. It is fatal to ask 'Do you doubt my integrity?' for that is a phrase used only by crooks. Trust is not something you can demand. It has to be earned over a period of years by a process which can begin with the first acquaintance. The final agreement is between friends. The same rule applies on the factory floor. The industrial dispute we aim to prevent is the one which would otherwise take place in five years' time. To check it at the outset we begin talking now, not about wage differentials but about racing, fishing, music, or chess. Once you have established yourself as a friend you can go on to prove that you are a man to be trusted.

Only after a proper relationship has been established can one frame the message to be conveyed. In each individual case the message will be different but let us assume hopefully that it is known exactly what is to be said. As from any management the message must be individual but from industry as a whole three messages need to be emphasised repeatedly. First, people need reminding that industry created the world in which we actually live; the world of the automobile, telephone, typewriter, and radio. Second, it must be reiterated that wealth must be made before it can be spent. Third, while business offers employment it does not exist for that purpose. Having noted this, it must be recalled that communication is a two-way process and that reaction has to be sensed and analysed. It is a sign of failure when a deputation comes to complain about something. We should have known about it beforehand. We should have been there first.

Come now to the importance of style, which is the imprint of character upon what we do and say. Any effective announcement or message conveys a sense of personality. While precise and terse, it goes beyond precision and brevity. It comes from a known character, not from a faceless management. It never includes long words and involved constructions. Short words are best, each one a hammer blow and not a handful of cotton wool. Last of all, it often includes a touch of humour. This serves more than one purpose. It makes the message human. It attracts attention. Above all, it assists memory. And the secret of humour, employed as a deliberate tool or device, is to tie in the joke with the message that remembering one means remembering both. This is not as easy as it may sound and success not derived from inspiration must result from hours and hours of work.

Why is communication so vital to industry? Because this is another example of the vacuum's importance. If we do not tell our own story it will be told for us by others and greatly to our disadvantage. In the world of today there is a wealth of information circulating on every subject. People are deluged with facts and theories and advice about everything, whether spoken, printed, or broadcast. No industrial group can afford to surround itself in mystery or find a special dignity in silence. It is that reticence which will make it vulnerable to allegations which will range from ill-treatment of its employees to pollution of the atmosphere, from waste of by-products to bribery in local government. Nor do we save the situation by denying the accusation. All we can do by such protest is to attract more attention to all that has been said against us. But the fault is ours. We created the vacuum into which all this nonsense had to flow. Bad instructions are sometimes deliberate, arising from some muddled motive, the desire to humiliate, the desire to reveal somebody's stupidity, the desire to show that the coming disaster was not our fault. In such instances the will to communicate is absent. More often, however, the will is there but the imagination is not.

Experience of this sort leads us to the general conclusion that the vacuum in human affairs may be more important than we have so far been led to suspect. A perceptive politician once referred to the winds of change and a far greater man, living in an earlier and greater period of history, once contrasted the beneficent gales of spring with the tempest which brings only destruction in its wake. But the hurricane which appears to blow the roof off a house has not really done so. The roof was actually sucked off by the vacuum formed in the building's lee. In human affairs the vacuum plays as significant a part and one no less vital for being so often unnoticed. We have been misled by historians who tell us of revolutions brought about by ill-nourished peasants plotting revolt against their masters. But people who are really oppressed never revolt and any revolution which is seemingly the result of discontent should always, on that supposition, have happened a great deal sooner when things were a great deal worse. Tyrants flourish and it is their well-meaning successors who face the firing squad. In other words we do wrong to waste time on studying the conspiracy but should rather concentrate our attention on the government which is to be overturned. Talk about the real or imagined suffering of the poor is irrelevant because each revolution is really brought about by the government itself, by the men who created the vacuum into which the rebels are almost unwillingly sucked. Will the present regimes in the West be destroyed by *coups d'état*? It would seem quite possible, but we should do wrong to ask ourselves whether the armed forces of the Western nations have any such plans in mind. They haven't and it would be of no great significance if they had. The people to study are the ministers and their immediate entourage. Is their ineptitude sufficient to create the vacuum into which some other force will be drawn?

What is true of internal stability or its absence is no less true of foreign affairs. We are apt to blame an aggressive nation for causing a war and there is a sense in which our strictures may be just. But what of the wretched country which is invaded? Its part in causing the war was probably far more important. It may not be morally to blame but it created the situation in which war had become inevitable. The Spanish conquest of Mexico shed far more light on Aztec weakness than upon Spanish resolution and courage, admitting as we must that Cortés had both. Empires collapse as a result of internal decay and rulers who are guiltless of any particular crime cause disaster through all

211

they have failed to do. An effective rule has direction, momentum, colour, and speed. It is the lack of these positive characteristics, as perhaps in Tsarist Russia, which must eventually create the vacuum. If the West is to survive it must achieve a measure of unity which is so far conspicuously lacking, but its failure, if it fails, will be in Brussels and Washington, not on the threatened frontier nor even in the countries which cling most desperately to that sovereign status they can no longer afford to maintain.

6 for success from BALLANTINE BOOKS Help yourself.